Confusion on
the Potomac

Confusion on the Potomac

THE ALARMING CHAOS AND FEUDS OF WASHINGTON • By **CARLISLE BARGERON**

Publishers **WILFRED FUNK, INC.** *New York*

Contents

I.	INSIDE WASHINGTON	1
II.	THE CITY OF CONFUSION	15
III.	WAR ON THE DOLLAR-A-YEAR MEN	30
IV.	THE HENDERSON-KNUDSEN CONFLICT	47
V.	BATTLE OF THE ECONOMISTS	71
VI.	LABOR LEADERS AND COMMUNISTS	103
VII.	THE ECCLES-MORGENTHAU FEUD	122
VIII.	CONFLICT IN THE SUPREME COURT	134
IX.	THE "GOOD-NEIGHBOR" MUDDLE	155
X.	ICKES, OIL, AND WAR-CONSCIOUSNESS	183
XI.	THE SATURNALIA OF BILLIONS	201
XII.	THE TRAGIC PLIGHT OF CONGRESS	217
XIII.	I BELIEVE IN AMERICA	244

Confusion on
the Potomac

CHAPTER I

Inside Washington

Washington is the most important capital in the world. In spite of this it is a mixture of Middle Western small-town provincialism and the pseudo-sophistication and exhibitionism of New York's Stork Club. With the exception of Wall Street in the roaring twenties, when a rumor that "Morgan was in the market" would cause a turnover of hundreds of thousands of shares, there is perhaps no other place in the country where a rumor travels faster and has more effect on the lives of people.

There is as much privacy in Washington as there is in hanging one's laundered clothes on a line to dry.

When a bad check bounces back on a Congressman, and one often does among the 435 of them, it is talked about by the banker at a dinner party and may end up in a gossip column; or if it doesn't, it might just as well, because of the circulation the story gets, anyway. Other bits of gossip travel equally fast. At a cocktail party, for instance, a vivacious matron, known for her caustic tongue and whose witticisms are well known throughout official circles, shoves a high ranking Army officer in the stomach and he loses his balance and falls on the floor. All Washington, with its pseudo sophistication giggles about it.

The wife of a government official just elevated to the $8,000 or $10,000 a year class, decides she must buy her clothes in New York and joins the gay party of wives which one may meet on any trip of the Congressional Limited leaving Washington at 4 o'clock. She chats animatedly on such subjects as the number of unemployed, the occupation of Martinique, and the maldistribution of gold.

The population of Washington, before the Second World War, was estimated at 600,000. It was still predominantly Middle Western and Southern, and is so still, despite the influx of New Yorkers with the advent of the New Deal. Everybody in Washington either works for the government or lives off those who do. The largest population is concentrated in the northwest residential section, which rises slowly from the downtown section, only six feet above sea level, and extends out Connecticut and Wisconsin avenues to perhaps a height of 200 feet.

The result is that official and semi-official Washington—lawmakers, members of the executive branch and journalists—work together by day and live together by night. One sees the same faces at parties, day in and day out; in most instances he sees the same waiters serving. It is like one overly large family living together, all talking and doing at the same time and getting on one another's nerves.

From seven o'clock in the morning until slightly past nine, because of the staggered hours at which government employees go to work, one sees apartment houses and residences belching forth a populace headed downhill to business, fairly concentrated in an area of twenty-two by eight blocks. Going home in the afternoon from 3:30 o'clock on, it is uphill, and in the winter if there is snow or sleet on the ground, there is a delay of two hours or longer as motorists try to get up over a slight hump at Florida and Connecticut avenues, or at Mount Alban. For 80 cents one rides in a taxi from the farthest northwest corner to the Capitol or the railroad station at the other edge of town.

In reasonable weather the Goodyear blimp floats lazily over the city, bearing a streamer telling of a clothing sale. It flies sightseers around the tip of the Washington monument, but the service caters to flying Congressmen and their friends without charge. Its main business is to lobby silently for congressional interest in lighter-than-air craft; to serve as a silent rebuke for those who became discouraged about the development of this type of aviation when disaster befell the dirigibles *Los Angeles* and *Shenandoah*.

The most widely read literature, according to surveys, is the "Personal Advice" column in the *Post* conducted by "Mary Haworth." Not syndicated and prepared conscientiously, it gives advice on people's most intimate problems—whether one woman should accept favors from another woman's husband, whether the girl should marry the boy before he goes off to camp.

[3]

Three clairvoyants do a comfortable business with the wives of government officials, Senators and Congressmen.

A minimum of thirteen political columnists in Washington's four newspapers chat along daily on what men of the government are doing and what they should do; while four others tell of the problems of the minor department heads and their employees, their comings and goings, a department head's favoritism for his pretty stenographer; the activities of the workers' committees. If your picture appears in one column, you can by arrangement between the *Times-Herald* and Blackstone, the florist, get a bouquet free.

The newspapers devote relatively more space to "society activities" than any other newspaper in the country. In addition to their ample coverage of engagements, weddings and parties, women columnists record the charm and whimsies and witty sayings of the men and women of their particular circle. There is such a columnist for nearly every segment of Washington life, and it is a pastime to watch the upward progress of one's fellow citizen from one column to another. The same people pretty much are written about every day. They are rated according to the column in which they appear.

When a new Dollar-a-Year man or a new government executive arrives in town, he is seized upon with the avidity with which the girls in a small town, used to going with the same fellows all their lives, grab a new male comer to their midst. And before he realizes what has happened, his whole life has been unfolded to the point of whether he likes grapefruit or cereal for breakfast.

Those whose business it is to know what is going on in Washington read these social columns closely to see who is entertaining whom, and why. In 1937, it was one of these columnists, Helen Essary on the *Times-Herald,* who casually told that Myron C. Taylor, head of United States Steel, and John L. Lewis were meeting. It was the first inkling of Taylor's signing a contract with the CIO, a very important event, indeed.

The garden party which the British ambassador and Lady Lindsay gave for the British King and Queen in 1939 bordered on being a flop, because some of the women columnists were not invited while one of them, related to Lady Lindsay, was. One of the neglected ones wrote that Queen Elizabeth was not all sweetness and kindness; that it could be very well understood how she manipulated Wally Simpson and Windsor off the throne.

The columnists, men and women, make a terrific impact upon small-townish Washington. They ring the full scale of men's vanities and prejudices, puffing those who impress them and disparaging those who do not. They play one man against another, one woman against another, and with everybody living so close together, there is the effect of a never-ending buzz.

The newcomer to Washington notes at once a sort of indefinable din, and gradually he perceives the overtone of the columnists. It ranges from the steady tom-

tom of Walter Lippmann, through the dramatics of Hugh Johnson, the baritone of Raymond Clapper, the machine-gun rattle of Drew Pearson and Robert S. Allen, to the high soprano of the women. Weaving through the cacophony are the argumentative notes of David Lawrence and Mark Sullivan, and always, in the final act, Westbrook Pegler draws his sword, and as the sun goes down in the evening, Dorothy Thompson screams like a banshee betokening death in the home. Ray Tucker and Paul Mallon, although widely syndicated, are not printed in Washington; but every newspaper has its own columnists to augment the voices of the syndicated writers.

On a large table in the National Press Club every afternoon there are 100 or so "statements" or government publicity releases known as "hand-outs" from which the newspapermen may cull those he is interested in. They come from the government's 1,000 or so publicity men, from the countless "trade" or "lobbying" organizations of virtually every industry in the United States, the farmers, big business men's organizations, organizations of not so big business men, of steel producers, of oil producers, liquor manufacturers, the beer trade, the soft-drink trade, the veterans of World War No. 1, the veterans of the Spanish-American War, from privately endowed "people's lobbies," from the organization seeking to bring about standardization of screws, to reform the calendar, and so on without end.

They are all a part of the propaganda din of Washington. One may learn at this table that there is an oil shortage, that there is no such thing as an oil shortage; that the Gregorian calendar is the best, that it is the worst; that the farmers and veterans and the wage earners are being coddled, that they are being abused. The table in itself constitutes a mute form, but the statements cease to be mute when they hit the headlines or are repeated on the radio.

A person does not have to prepare a statement or write a column to be a part of the propaganda factory. He can drop an idea at a luncheon table and it will have made the rounds of the city and come back to smack him in the face in the Press Club's taproom or in the Mayflower Hotel cocktail room or at the Shoreham that night.

Washington lives on lungs and ideas. Relate a story to a Congressman, he will relate it to his colleagues in the cloakrooms. As likely as not it will bob up presently in a speech. In the days of more tolerance in the Washington ballyhoo, when the philosophy of "live and let live" was more the order among those who make their living by their wits, it was not uncommon for an outright quack to get nation-wide publicity by visiting a White House secretary and, when he came away, leaving the impression that he had discussed his momentous proposal with the President. The New Dealers are more cautious about permitting the White House to be used as a sounding board.

In the early New Deal a highly stationed governmental official blew up and resigned and made known

that he had a scandal to reveal. To inquiring newspapermen the White House attachés said, as if it hurt
them, that while they couldn't be quoted, the truth
was that this fellow had been annoying the associates
in his department, and that his real complaint was that
he wanted to be appointed minister to a small European Court.

The result was that this man was laughed out of
town. Congressmen and newspapermen alike heard the
story about him, and his revelation, which had some
credibility at least, could get no audience. This man
had been prominent in politics. The last heard of him,
he had on shoes rundown at the heels, a worn-out brief
case, and was trying bitterly to get up a movement to
"stop Roosevelt."

The queer thing about the story circulated against
him was that he was urged to accept a place in the
Reconstruction Finance Corporation, which is noted
for its pretty and numerous girls. In Washington men
were occasionally given pretty much the same propaganda treatment which the Germans gave Hess when
he first landed in Scotland—the circulation of stories
that he was crazy.

Washington, thus far described, is not peculiar to
the New Deal. It is ever the home of gossip, conflict
and backbiting. But in the days agone these did not
have so much effect on the lives of millions of citizens
because their government was not so concentrated.
The advent of the New Deal stepped up the tempo,
and imposition of the defense structure on top of this

stepped up the tempo further. Along with this, Washington journalism became franker. Herbert Hoover, when he was President, complained of the developing tendency to subordinate principles to personalities in the written accounts of issues. The personal element had been there before, but it was not so frankly written about. Formerly Senators could make impassioned speeches for consumption back home and then tell their colleagues in the cloakroom they hadn't meant a word they said, without this appearing in the papers. Official Washington is less interested in the principle of a particular bill a Senator introduces or a statement he makes, or the effect it will have on the commonweal, than in how it bears on his particular ambition. What is he up to? Just as a town of 20,000 people hears with interest of a man getting a promotion in the bank, so Washington looks upon the actions of its public men. They are fellow townspeople.

In Washington in 1941, men were varyingly classified as New Dealers, Liberals, Conservatives, Left-wingers and Communists, instead of Republicans and Democrats of the past. Business men from New York and elsewhere were constantly seeking to learn whether a man just appointed in the government was a "Leftist" or "Rightist." It really meant very little difference. The over-all term "bureaucrat" would have been more informative.

Beneath the surface of the Washington government were thousands and thousands of the routine government employees, men and women, who entered the service because it afforded them a comfortable living, away from the uncertainties of private employment, and a comfortable pension when they became old. But on top of this, in the Hoover days, in the Coolidge days, still farther back, were the more ambitious department heads whose desire was to perpetuate their agencies and increasingly add to their importance. Just as doctors, lawyers, actors, scientists and the like want to advance their professions, there was never a time when a government bureaucrat, if he was worth his salt, did not want to increase his stature by adding to his authority and importance, and to do this he must enforce more government on the people.

The only difference was, that in the changing times, just as men in other vocations had had their place in the sun, the bureaucrat had come to have his. It meant very little difference essentially whether he professed a belief in the "capitalistic" system or "socialism," or whether he was a conservative or a liberal or a leftist. Being human, he was for entrenching himself in authority and increasing that authority. This meant, of course, a tightening control by the government over people, and whether that control meant socialism, fascism or communism, was largely rhetorical.

The genus Bureaucrat even in the days of Jefferson wanted the government to "do something for and with" the people, and let his agency be the one to do it. But down over the years in the development of government "of the people, for the people and by the people," lawyers predominated in the lawmaking—to such an extent, indeed, that editors and educators, non-legal minds generally, often thought they saw a huge conspiracy on the part of the lawyer-lawmakers to make laws for the other lawyers to break.

With the advent of the New Deal a distinct new type was brought into the executive branch. College professors, economists, monetary experts, sociologists, came to Washington in droves. Scientific minds had long worked in the various departments, but they were subordinated to the political forces. Now, however, they were to become aggressive, to become policy makers. They were to dominate the government. Generally speaking, they constituted the New Dealers. They were referred to as "brilliant minds" and "intellectuals," admiringly by their friends, derisively by their critics. Certainly they were active minds.

As their socio-political movement swept out over the country they absorbed lesser political movements or made "tie-ups" with them—labor organizations, farm organizations, and state political organizations. In addition to the army of government workers in Washington, there are more than 1,000,000 Federal employees out over the country. They reach down into the smallest hamlets. But in the past they were not politically obligated to one group in Washington. In one state they might form the political machine of a Senator, in a community, of a Congressman or a political leader who held no job in the government. But the New Deal movement progressed rapidly to absorb them, to make these million or so workers obligated to it.

This setup comprised the "vast propaganda machine" against which New Deal critics frequently inveighed. In Washington a leader expressed an idea, a denunciation of a political enemy, a boost for a friend or for government action in a particular field, and almost with the rapidity of lightning it swept over the country. Aside from the established channels of communication, the legions of New Dealers in the field took up the chant. Many state governors and still more mayors became beholden to the Washington New Dealers, which meant their millions of state government workers became a part of the gigantic machine.

In Washington nearly all of the departments had a news ticker. A Senator sounded-off in the Senate chamber and immediately it was flashed on the news tickers around town. Perhaps the Senator said there were not as many men unemployed as was being claimed by those who wanted appropriations to support them, and promptly other and contentious voices entered the debate from their respective places uptown. In the National Press Club, the ticker reported that a Senator had just attacked Harold Ickes or Madame Perkins. Groups of newspapermen would thereupon hie themselves to the offices of Ickes or the Secretary of Labor to hear what they had to say. Similarly, the tickers reported briefly that the Secretary of Commerce had just taken some action which the newspapermen recognized as being in conflict with what the Secretary of Agriculture had been advocating. Here was a "clash" which made news. The more outstanding government officials held press conferences at stated periods. In addition, the ticker carried the information that the State Department or some other department had called a press conference for 11 o'clock, for 3 o'clock, or, in some instances, immediately.

It was essential for an ambitious man, or one who didn't want to be swept completely out of the fast-moving parade, to make himself heard through the collective megaphone. And it had its limitations. The newspaper headlines are only eight columns wide, the radio cannot operate more than twenty-four hours a day. The struggle for expression in this limited space made Washington pretty much of a bedlam in normal times; necessarily, more so as the contentious forces were added to. It behooved the economist seeking recognition to work out startling statistics to support his idea; the other active minds had to prepare sensational themes. Truth about the government became virtually impossible to obtain.

In 1941, defense workers—in important positions and in purely clerical capacities—were being added to the vociferous hodgepodge at the rate of 1,500 or so a week. In no single department was it possible to learn the over-all figure. Business men arrived at the rate of 3,000 a day and fought for hotel accommodations. People were routed out of their apartments as the government took them over for office space. In many instances, stenographers worked in bathrooms of former private dwellings. Taxicabs were hard to get; people had to stand in line at the more popular-priced restaurants; local officials struggled with the increasing traffic problem. The movies and department stores did a land-office business, as did the cocktail rooms. Bartenders were imported from Baltimore.

In a period of eight months there were nineteen unsolved rape cases, and Mrs. Roosevelt at a press conference warned young women not to have a drink with a man whom they did not know very well. A Washington newspaper with graphs and drawings advised how women could protect themselves with hatpins.

CHAPTER II

The City of Confusion

IN PARIS, in the spring of 1940, self-seeking politicians
and the self-seeking influences behind them wrote the
final chapter in their Book of Free France. Not even
the approach of the traditional enemy could unite
them or bring back together the disjointed republic of
their creation.

In 1941, Washington, a city originally fashioned by
the Frenchman L'Enfant even to surpass his beloved
city on the Seine, presented a frightening similarity to
the Paris of 1940. Fervent speakers were periodically
beseeching unity on the part of the American people.
Young men were being taken from their homes into
training camps; housewives were being urged to sacrifice.

But in the city on the Potomac, described affection-
ately these many years as ten miles square of glistening
masonry and wide avenues, the scene was one of confusion, of backbiting and bickering, of the conflict
of selfish interests and selfish ambitions.

The New Dealers and Dollar-a-Year men were figuratively as embattled as were the Federals and Confed-

erates at Bull Run; the New Dealers were fighting among themselves; the Dollar-a-Year men were quarreling in their own camp. Men in high places were not speaking to one another if they could avoid it; "office politics" was the order of the day.

Instead of moving in one direction against Hitler, Washington's overbulging bureaucracy proceeded like the multiple-armed octopus. Groups sought to undermine other groups, and individuals sought to undermine other individuals.

Washington in 1941 was a concentration of men's energies and their selfish ambitions, the product of which inevitably was an overwhelming confusion.

After the presidential campaign of 1940, the New Dealers returned to Washington from the hustings, so to speak, to survey their victory. Some of them had been in New York working to bring about Mr. Roosevelt's election to a third term, others had been in Chicago and elsewhere. But even those who had retained their stations in Washington had been engaged in the campaign to the exclusion of everything else. To the accompanying derision of political experts, they had accomplished what American history said could not be done. Now, they contemplated the sky as the only limit to their zeal and their plans.

Then suddenly, as they rubbed their dazzled eyes, a startling picture confronted them. Some 200 industrialists and business men had, in their absence, moved into Washington and seemingly taken over the world's greatest spending spree, the Saturnalia of Billions, dressed up as National Defense. It was a picture to cause consternation in the New Dealers' reforming ranks. It was, indeed, about as alarming a situation as ever smote a group of intense men.

Collective high blood pressure had come to them before—back in 1939 when Mr. Roosevelt's preoccupation with the European war became pronounced. This had not been on the program when they set out with him in 1933 to effect revolutionary reforms. They had had a definite understanding, instead, that come what may in Europe, their Chief "would not make the mistake of Woodrow Wilson" and permit himself to be diverted from his domestic program. That this was a great mistake on Wilson's part, the New Dealers had contended from the day they poured off the incoming trains to close the nation's banks and begin the remaking of the economic structure from the bottom up.

Mr. Roosevelt early showed his agreement with them by expressing his contempt for European politics and politicians. Early in his administration he torpedoed the London economic conference. He chided England and France for spending so much on armaments and frankly told friends that he knew European politicians and did not intend to be hoodwinked by them. Before his inauguration he stopped at Washington en route to Warm Springs, Georgia, to confer with the retiring President, Herbert Hoover, at the latter's request. Mr. Hoover urged him to join in a statement saying that the Hoover administration's foreign policy, which included support of impending international conferences, would be continued. Mr. Roosevelt refused, and Washington newspapermen who accompanied him on to Warm Springs were impressed by the assertion of his aides, Ray Moley, who was then his closest confidant and had participated in the meetings with Mr. Hoover; the late W. H. Woodin, who was to be Mr. Roosevelt's first Secretary of the Treasury, and Sumner Welles, later to become Under-Secretary of State, that it was up to Europe to work out her own problems; that if the new administration entered into any bargaining it would be with a view to collection of the debts owed by Britain and France. Welles had long cherished a hope of making "hemisphere solidarity" the keynote of this country's foreign policy. Woodin, a delightful gentleman, drawn suddenly from the presidency of the American Car and Foundry, fascinated at being suddenly taken into the company of the "great," an idolater of Mr. Roosevelt, would chuckle and repeat over and over to the newspapermen on the special train:

"Those European statesmen have met their master now."

Then, after he took office, one of Mr. Roosevelt's first major acts was to take this country off the gold standard, a step that for years was to cost him the friendship of Senator Carter Glass of Virginia. The principal effect of it was to place this country in a better competitive position with Britain in the world markets. Continuing this attitude toward Europe, Mr. Roosevelt encouraged the investigation by a Senate committee known as the Nye Committee in 1935, of the munitions industry and the causes of this country's entrance into the First World War. Day after day, the committee laid the blame at the door of "international bankers" and "munitions makers," and assiduously immunized the American people against being "duped again." As a result of the revelations of this committee, Congress enacted the Neutrality Act, which, as amended two years later, prohibited any American citizen from trading with a nation at war, and any American merchant vessel from entering a war zone. Senator Nye, who sponsored the legislation, has repeatedly said that Mr. Roosevelt gave him the idea for it. Nye, at that time, was a New Dealer.

But the New Dealers had a momentary fright that the President was becoming "European minded," as they put it, in late 1937, when in a speech at Chicago he demanded that aggressor nations be quarantined. Traveling with the presidential party at the time was Ernest Lindley, a New Deal journalist, the President's campaign biographer, and an intimate friend of the Roosevelts. He was so angry over what he thought the speech betokened that he shook his fist at Jimmy Roosevelt and exclaimed in almost these words:

"I said long ago that if your father would stay out of European affairs he would go down in history as this country's greatest President. But I also said I doubted he would stay out."

It developed, however, that the New Dealers' perturbation on this occasion was unwarranted. Mr. Roosevelt was concerned about the furore that had been created by the revelation that his recent appointee to the Supreme Court, Hugo L. Black, was a member of the Ku Klux Klan. He wanted to get the Black incident out of the public's consciousness, and at the last minute inserted the "quarantine" reference in his speech, unknown to the State Department, at the instance of Harold L. Ickes, whose knowledge of men and affairs ranges all the way from the treatment of dictators to that of mere citizens who make jack-rabbit starts in their automobiles.

But when, with the outbreak of the war in September 1939, Mr. Roosevelt immediately linked this country's destiny with the democracies and took steps to aid them, the indignation of his young disciples knew no bounds.

"There," they exclaimed, "he goes!"

They took it to mean the end of their day in the sun—the end of the honeymoon of Intellectuals, Professors and Economists. Conservative business men and industrialists would now return to the scene, they assumed, and replace them in the President's councils. They groped for stronger epithets than Conservative, Reactionary and Fascist. For several weeks their feeling was as intense as that of the Communists with whom they had worked for the greater part of eight years. They joined with the Communists in denouncing William C. Bullitt, American Ambassador to Paris, as the arch instigator of the war!

Bullitt, member of a wealthy and aristocratic Philadelphia family, had never been one of the New Dealers. Instead, he was an adventurer in international politics. As a young man he went to Europe on the famous Ford Peace Ship of the First World War and he became a protégé of the noted pacifist, Madame Schwimmer. From the Versailles Peace Conference, Woodrow Wilson sent him to study the permanency of the new Bolshevik government in Russia. Afterwards he returned to the United States, and through sensational testimony before the Senate Foreign Relations Committee he became largely instrumental in scuttling the treaty of Versailles and Wilson's dream of a League of Nations. He was out of the limelight thereafter, until Mr. Roosevelt resurrected him and named him as our first ambassador to the Soviets. At Moscow he tried to tell Stalin how to run his government. Being unsuccessful, he became fed up with the Communists and was subsequently sent to Paris.

Bullitt has denied promising the Polish Ambassador we would enter the war, and other charges that he urged the French leaders to challenge Hitler when the latter moved into Poland. He has even exhibited a letter from the then French Premier, Daladier, stating that Bullitt held out no promises of aid to him. But the New Dealers, in their state of mind in the fall of '39, were prepared to think anything of this highly emotional man. Their remarks about him and even about Mr. Roosevelt would not bear reprinting. No stronger imprecations or profanity were ever spoken against their enemies in America's Class War. It was a question for several weeks whether they would not openly break with the President as the Communists did.

The irony of the New Dealers' charges against Bullitt is that after he had returned home, after the fall of France, they circulated reports that he was an appeaser because he wanted to send food to the republic in whose downfall he had undoubtedly played an important part. An example of his emotionalism is given in a conversation Secretary of State Cordell Hull had with a friend just before Bullitt sailed for home. The friend asked Hull how Bullitt was getting along, and Hull replied with a grimace, "He's over there with a machine gun in his lap."

The New Dealers' state of mind can be better appreciated when it is realized that one of the strongest denunciations of war and particularly of Britain and what was described as her "divide and rule" policy to be made over the past ten years was contained in a book published in 1938 by Jerome Frank, one of their leaders. Frank felt embittered for several weeks, then came to the support of the President's policy and waited for the day when he would be given the security of a Federal judgeship.

Older counsel—Harold Ickes, Harry Hopkins, Felix Frankfurter, and Robert H. Jackson, who was a conscientious objector in the last war—moved among the dissenters and applied cold towels to their heated brows. The younger men had gone off half-cocked, the elders explained. Because of the economic situation in this country it didn't look as though they could remain in office unless Mr. Roosevelt embraced the European war as a vehicle for re-election. They explained, the calmer men did, how vast defense expenditures could be used to carry on the New Deal domestic program. Without the defense spending the New Deal seemed to be stopped. Wasn't this apparent to the hotheads, the leaders asked? Just a few weeks before the outbreak of war, the conservatives in Congress had succeeded in defeating a huge spending bill—the so-called four-billion-dollar spend-lease appropriation by which the country was to be given another injection. Without a revival of government spending in some form, the New Deal seemed jeopardized.

Also, it was explained to the younger men, they were all wrong in their belief that they were to be replaced. They were given assurances that they were to remain in the saddle, that they would become the defense experts, and have bigger funds to spend than they had ever dreamed of.

But this realistic political thinking was not confined to the New Dealers. Several weeks before the nominating conventions, Herbert Hoover met secretly in Washington with Republican leaders—Senators McNary, Taft and Vandenberg, and the minority leader of the House, Joe Martin. Senator Styles Bridges was away making a speech. These gentlemen pessimistically discussed the effect the defense expenditures would have on the campaign, particularly in the highly industrialized East and East-Central states. They agreed they had had Roosevelt defeated. Now it was doubtful.

During the bickering in Mr. Roosevelt's official family, he had called in a committee of industrialists headed by Edward S. Stettinius, chairman of the board of the United States Steel Corporation, to make a study of how to gear up the country's industry to defense needs. The high light of its report was a recommendation that the New Deal hold up on further reform, that certain reform measures already effected be repealed, and that the defense production job be placed in the hands of experienced industrialists or a group similar to the War Industries Board of the last war.

This committee and its findings excited the New Dealers. If they were to remain in the saddle, how about this committee, they demanded. Mr. Roosevelt's reassuring answer was to send Stettinius and his committee home and to shelve their report. Thus a New Deal family war was averted. The New Dealers put aside their apprehensions and joined wholeheartedly in the all-out crusade for Britain. Their affection for the Communists turned into hate. The latter continued to follow Stalin's party line; the New Dealers fell in behind Roosevelt's.

So it can be imagined how consternated they were in November and December of 1940, when, their work of re-electing Mr. Roosevelt finished, they found business and industrial interlopers in their nests!

In the heat of the campaign Mr. Roosevelt had brought Stettinius back. He had brought in William S. Knudsen, production wizard of the automobile industry; John D. Biggers, president of Libbey-Owens-

Ford Glass Company; William L. Batt, of the ball-bearing industry; Donald Nelson, vice president and chairman of the executive committee of Sears, Roebuck and Averell Harriman, Chairman of the board of Union Pacific. And they, in turn, had brought in scores of less publicized Dollar-a-Year men. Like a heavily laden tree, they were clustered all over the defense superstructure that was rapidly being thrown up.

On the eve of the Republican convention at Philadelphia, Mr. Roosevelt had named a Republican, the aging Henry Stimson, to be Secretary of War, and another Republican, Frank Knox, to be Secretary of the Navy. The New Dealers had assumed that the appointment of these two men as well as the calling in of men like Stettinius and Knudsen, was necessary political strategy, and that they would be dismissed or blanketed by New Dealers when the campaign was over.

But their first effort in this direction failed and threw them into a panic. They learned that Stimson and Knox, for example, not only were to remain but were insisting on naming their own aides. The plan to blanket Knox was the placing of Tommy Corcoran as Assistant Secretary of the Navy. This man, just turning forty, had emerged from the obscurity of a law clerk in the Reconstruction Finance Corporation, to become one of the spark plugs of the New Deal. In this capacity he resigned from his government job in October to campaign for Mr. Roosevelt from New York City. He had been a New Deal master mind. Now he told his followers that he thought he rated a title of dignity and rank, something that would give more tangibility to his amazing career. Frankfurter and Ickes supported him. But Knox remained unmoved.

Becoming worried over the persistent campaign in Corcoran's behalf, Knox went to the President for a reaffirmation of their understanding that he could appoint his own aides. He got this reaffirmation, but he again became worried when the campaign on behalf of Corcoran continued. Then members of the House Appropriations Committee exposed Corcoran's lobbying activities to build up some wealth in the weeks intervening between the end of the campaign and his reassumption of governmental office. These revelations fortified Knox in his determination not to take Corcoran into his office, and also killed off the latter's chances of getting any other place of prominence that required confirmation by the Senate.

Early one day in the spring there arrived in Washington what is known in the trade as a wildcat oil promoter. He had sunk several hundred thousand dollars in a well in Alaska. He hadn't yet struck oil and he was out of funds. He wanted the Reconstruction Finance Corporation to finance him. He had been told that the best person for him to see was Corcoran. Within a short while after they met, Corcoran decided that the procedure would be first to get the Navy to certify the drilling project as essential to National Defense. Then he took the problem to his friend Ickes, under whose jurisdiction Alaska comes. Ickes called Knox and asked him over to lunch in Ickes' pretentious quarters in the Interior Building, comprising not only a private bath and dining room but a private bedroom. On one occasion when he was thought to be ill in Naval Hospital, Ickes, instead, was administering his department from his bedroom right there in the building.

Ickes put the proposition up to Knox, and the latter told him to write a letter about it. Ickes got the impression that Knox was unfriendly, so his letter was very formal and put the responsibility squarely upon Knox. Not satisfied with his carefully worded letter, Ickes had one of his aides call the Navy Secretary on the telephone to emphasize that the decision would have to be solely his.

Inasmuch as the transaction did not go through, and no publicity had attended it, the significant thing to Ickes was that when he appeared, a few weeks later, before a secret session of the House Appropriations Committee, the Republican members knew every detail of it. There was a heated exchange of words between Ickes and these Republicans, but the Democratic members of the committee voted to suppress it on the ground that it was an attempt to smear a cabinet officer. Ickes held Knox responsible for his experience before the committee, and afterwards he would only speak to Knox when he had to. This incident was to affect their relations as they met at cabinet meetings thereafter to determine this country's course in a war-torn world.

The word spread through the New Dealers' ranks that their ebullient and resourceful leader, Corcoran, was out. It apparently betokened ill for the rest of them. Their excitement became intense.

It was in an effort to quiet the New Dealers that Mr. Roosevelt, when he went off on a Caribbean cruise just after the campaign, took both Hopkins and Ickes with him. These two had been bitter rivals ever since the New Deal came in, and for a couple of years Ickes had been preaching in New Deal ranks that Hopkins was losing his New Dealism and playing ball with industrialists and business men. So Mr. Roosevelt took both of them along.

When he returned to Washington the excitement was at its height. Then, as he sought to give more definite form to the defense setup, Leon Henderson, who was later to become the country's price controller, was left dangling in an off-side post. Corcoran was out altogether. Dollar-a-Year men seemed to have the upper hand in the defense program. Hell broke loose in Washington!

Henderson sulkingly left town. The remaining New Dealers declared open war on the Dollar-a-Year men. They set out to apply against Stettinius, Knudsen, Biggers, and the men of their school of thought, the same propaganda and smearing tactics with which they had, over a period of eight years, advanced their class war.

They moved first against Stettinius and then they turned against Knudsen as more symbolic.

This campaign was to continue for months, right on through the summer of 1941, and to affect the lives of millions of citizens seeking to conduct their businesses, to educate their children, and in general to carry on their existence. It was to make of Washington a bedlam of confusion and jeopardize this country's preparation for war abroad or defense at home, whatever the need might develop to be.

CHAPTER III

War on the Dollar-a-Year Men

ALL GOVERNMENTS have to resort to pageantry, symbols and propaganda to deal with the rising and falling passions of their people. Our country, with its freedom of speech, is particularly given to heated controversies and agitations which attain a high pitch and then die out. Some seemingly go on forever; others smolder to flare up again; tenets from some sound controversies gain general acceptance.

But if a government were to respond to them simply because they are noisy, or because at the moment they actually seem to be the demands of a people, there would be but little if any stability in the people's affairs. Thus Herbert Hoover, when an agitation became too hot for him to ignore, had a way of creating a commission to "study" it or in some way to quiet or dissipate it. Occasionally the treatment was effective; more often, in his case, as was true of prohibition, it added to his troubles.

Mr. Roosevelt, when he returned from his Caribbean trip, was confronted with about as crucial a situation as ever existed in this country. For several years the nation had been rent by class strife. The major issue of his campaign had been that he would bend Hitler to his knees and would do it without Labor having to "sacrifice its social gains." The issue against Wendell Willkie was that, while he personally might feel pretty strongly about Hitler inasmuch as he kept saying he did, "those damned isolationist" Republicans would hamstring him. And Willkie himself was seemingly doubtful that he could both lick Hitler and "preserve Labor's social gains."

While Mr. Roosevelt was away in the Caribbean, the influences that had been most vociferously against him, that had accused him of wanting to be a dictator, that had accused him of spending away the country's substance, set up a persistent clamor for him to "assume the leadership" with money as no object in the war on that "fiend across the sea." His response when he got back to Washington was to send to Congress the seven-billion-dollar lend-lease bill with which we would underwrite Britain's needs in this country—regardless of whether we got any of the money back. Those who asked about that point were said to be thinking in terms of "silly dollars." This lend-lease bill was Mr. Roosevelt's way of "assuming the leadership." The vigor of the assumption may be gleaned from the fact that the night before the bill went to Congress it called for three billion dollars. With such a stroke of vigorous leadership as must have made Napoleon turn over in his grave, Harry Hopkins scratched out the "three" and made it a "seven." Six months later, while the

President was asking Congress for another six billion, it was to develop that less than $400,000,000 had actually been spent and the great bulk of this was for agricultural products.

Then, by way of socking Hitler again and at the same time "preserving Labor's social gains," the Office of Production Management (OPM) was created with Knudsen and Sidney Hillman as co-directors. Well, a body regardless of how contentious, could hardly want a more reassuring pageant than that—Knudsen the production genius driving America's unlimited production capacity to the hilt, and going right along at his side and protecting Labor's "social gains"—Sidney Hillman. The pageantry of it was enough to take a populace's breath. But it didn't.

The country's production leaders and editors were worried. Who was going to be the head man of the two? One of them had to be. There couldn't be two bosses. At least the employers had never heard of any such setup being effective.

If the "Big Dane" felt any hurt he never showed it. Instead he rose to the occasion and set out to assure his fellow industrialists that the arrangement was perfectly satisfactory to him. He and Hillman got along splendidly, he insisted. Moving rapidly among his associates in the business world, he worked enthusiastically at dispelling their apprehensions. The President had given him 100 per cent support, and he was satisfied he would continue to receive such support, he declared.

Regardless of how this man was to fare in the future, regardless of what he was to be able to accomplish, the story of Washington in the aftermath will very likely reveal him as a simon-pure, unalloyed patriot. His Danish background gave him a healthy respect for government—*the* Government. He could never bring himself to the role of critic. He was more inclined to look upon himself as a servant of government, particularly in those times, than look upon the government as his servant. The sacrifice he made in pride, in his just due of authority, in matters that bore on his reputation as a production genius, in an effort to present a harmonious picture to the country, afford a drastic commentary on the unsavory experience that lay in store for him.

In setting up Knudsen and Hillman with co-ordinate authority, Mr. Roosevelt undoubtedly thought he would satisfy his labor followers, who had voted so heavily for him in the campaign, and the conservatives whose support he now needed in the interest of "unity." But he entirely overlooked the problem of the New Deal politicos. Regardless of how well the Production Man and Labor Leader might be able to work together, the fact remained that under this arrangement Knudsen would parcel out most of the jobs. It meant that the Dollar-a-Year men and their kind would get the jobs.

For the New Dealers it was an intolerable situation. They immediately set out to check up on the antecedents of every Dollar-a-Year man in the city, and with the information they gathered they launched a smear campaign purporting to show that the industrialists were simply on hand to get business for their particular firms. Undoubtedly this was true in many instances. The human race doesn't change overnight. A more general selfish motivation of firms which lend the services of their officials to the government, however, is not to take advantage of a competitor so much as to see that they are not unfairly dealt with. In this instance, their motivation was relatively unimportant. There was certainly enough business to go around. Part of the propaganda against industrialists in 1940 and the first few months of 1941 was that some of them were refusing government contracts. This appears ridiculous when it is realized that the business of a business is to make money.

But on the strength of the charge that the Dollar-a-Year men only had selfish reasons for being in Washington, resolutions were introduced in the Senate to investigate them. One was by Senator Harry S. Truman of Missouri, who worked with the New Dealers; the other was by Senator Bennett Clark of Missouri, anti-New Dealer. Inasmuch as it is the unvarying rule that the Senator whose resolution is adopted shapes the direction of the investigation, a tug-of-war ensued between New Dealers and anti-New Dealers over which resolution should be adopted. The New Dealers won, and Truman promptly turned investigators loose on the Dollar-a-Year men. The direction this investigation took may be guessed from the fact that several months later, in mid-August, the report was circulated around Washington that the Dollar-a-Year men would be definitely exposed the following Tuesday. On this day, August 13, the committee counsel, Hugh A. Fulton, reported that out of $13,945,000,000 defense contracts on April 30, a total of $2,882,000,000 had been awarded to firms whose former employees were connected with OPM, and of these firms seven had been awarded a total of $2,619,000,000. He named these firms as the Bethlehem Steel Company, Chrysler Motors, Curtiss-Wright Company, General Electric Corporation, General Motors Corporation, United Aircraft Corporation, and United States Steel Corporation. The disclosure could scarcely be termed sensational. Senator Tom Connally of Texas remarked that it revealed "no vice" if the employee involved "uses no undue influence and if the industry offers the best contract." But in the intervening months the Dollar-a-Year men had been under suspicion, and as one controversy after another arose, several had been dismissed and others had returned to their businesses because of disgust. The agitation of the New Dealers, even after a few weeks, had become so hot that Mr. Roosevelt issued orders that every Dollar-a-Year man had to be approved by him. The result of this order was that many men who wanted to help out in the defense program were turned down on charges of the New Dealers that they had "bad" labor policies or were not properly "social conscious."

This, however, was only one phase of the attack. Against Knudsen, as the symbol of the Dollar-a-Year men, it was avowedly directed toward diminishing his reputation as a production genius. He had wholly detached himself from General Motors, where his salary in 1939, according to income-tax reports, was more than $300,000 a year. By continually harping on his shortcomings, real or fancied, and those of the OPM of which he was co-director, the attack had succeeded by midsummer in making his name pretty much of a household word throughout the country, and in each household had created at least a doubt as to whether he was the man for the job.

Throughout the spring and summer Washington literally seethed with stories of Knudsen's having fallen down on the job. Business men coming to the city, and falling victims of the confusion, heard the stories about Knudsen and were inclined to blame him for their own experiences. They returned to their communities to tell of the Washington bedlam and the stories they heard about Knudsen, thus adding to the circulation these stories were enjoying in the usual propaganda avenues. When, in midsummer, reports circulated all over the city that OPM was to be reorganized, there was never any suggestion that Knudsen's authority or stature in the defense program was to be increased. It was more of a question whether he would remain in the setup at all.

The uncertainty about Knudsen's tenure, in itself, added to the confusion. The Dollar-a-Year men whose numbers had increased to 500 in the OPM alone, and the approximately 2,000 employees of the OPM were kept in a constant state of demoralization.

In their earlier campaign against Knudsen, the New Dealers prepared figures to show that Eastern and East-Central states were getting the bulk of the defense business. Naturally this was so. These figures they took to Congress to stir up hostility toward the business men among the Mid-Western and Southern members. They succeeded. It was this, in fact, that oiled the way for the Truman investigation. Senator Kenneth D. McKellar, of Tennessee, an unblushing follower of the Andrew Jackson doctrine that to the victor belong the spoils, introduced a bill to run the business men out of town. His bill provided that the defense production job be put in the hands of younger men who would receive $6,000 or $7,000 a year. Coinciding with his action, a movement was launched in the House to investigate these men who had swept into Washington and, as the New Dealers described it, "gobbled up all the eight years' accomplishments of the New Deal."

Although the attack centered on Knudsen, it was not confined to him. It engulfed Stettinius and Knudsen's deputy, John D. Biggers, president of the Libbey-Owens-Ford Glass Company of Toledo, Ohio. Against Stettinius, it was of such a nature that a friend of twenty years' standing was moved to write an article in the *Saturday Evening Post* in defense of him. The article denied stories which it said had been circulated against Stettinius that he was a stuffed shirt and that his father had pushed him to the top in the industrial world. Instead, he was a man, the article said, who worked his way up notwithstanding his wealth, and whose greatest ambition was to help others.

Against Biggers it was charged, for example, that he was trying to meddle in Ohio politics, specifically that he was trying to push the appointment of a friend, an anti-New Dealer, for the politically powerful post of Collector of Internal Revenue in northwest Ohio.

An example of the attack against him was a story reported in the column of Jay Franklin which was sold to newspapers on the representation that it was a New Deal column. This story charged Biggers with trying to "play business politics in the OPM." It reported that Biggers and his associates considered Knudsen to be "a naïve, honest, simple man, and we must protect him."

A few days after this story was circulated, Franklin wrote an apology to Biggers and said he had been 40 per cent wrong. But Biggers was to continue for many months as the pet aversion of the New Dealers. For the first time in his life he was experiencing something that his sunshine, everybody-get-along-together philosophy couldn't cope with. His whole career had been built upon getting along with people, with the man under him and the man over him. He started out as a young Chamber of Commerce secretary in Detroit, moved to Toledo in a similar capacity, and rapidly shot to the top. As the president of Libbey-Owens he got $60,000 a year. He was lured off to Washington to direct the unemployment census in 1937, and he got along with the contentious forces so well that he was highly complimented and even turned back part of the appropriation that had been granted him. His success in the City of Conflict undoubtedly prompted him to come back when the call again came. It came from the President by way of Harry Hopkins.

Back in 1938 when Hopkins was elevated to the Secretaryship of Commerce to escape a Senate investigation of his administration of the WPA, brought on by the President's attempted purge campaigns of that year, he made a speech saying he really wanted Business and Government to get along together. The business men, by and large, were cynical. But there were four exceptions. They were Biggers, Batt, Harriman, and Nelson. The four of them had served pretty much from the beginning of the New Deal on the so-called Business Advisory Council set up in the Department of Commerce and in other capacities. They served patiently through the ridicule of their business associates, who asked just who paid any attention to their advice.

These four men, with Knudsen and Stettinius, were the first so-called Dollar-a-Year men on the scene. Naturally the others who flocked in were mostly men they tapped. Knudsen, Stettinius and Biggers were given the three top jobs. So the attack of the New Dealers centered on them.

None of them had ever experienced anything like it. Undoubtedly, Biggers in Toledo had aroused jealousies as he took over the leadership of the Community Club, as he became a trustee of the Boys' Club, as his name was always appearing in the papers in connection

with this and that civic activity, as his daughter and
daughter-in-law bobbed up in the rotogravures. But
these jealousies were not reflected in the papers. The
attacks on Stettinius and Biggers added to the demoralization of OPM.

Neither Knudsen nor Biggers nor Stettinius knew
anything about the political mechanics of Washington.
They couldn't comprehend them. They backed and
filled. They didn't know how to fight back in this sea
of propaganda. Experienced in the ways of business,
able to take care of themselves as their success in this
field demonstrated, this thing struck them as so utterly
fantastic as to be almost unbelievable.

Knudsen, Stettinius and Biggers tried to bring in
their own publicity men, but the New Dealers wouldn't
let them. Instead, in the OPM building was a publicity
staff of more than 200 persons under the direction of
Robert P. Horton, a former Scripps-Howard newspaperman. He worked under the Office of Emergency
Management, manned by New Dealers. Under the circumstances he and his men performed only a routine
and impersonal publicity job for Knudsen and his
OPM aides. Sidney Hillman, on the other hand, was
permitted a staff personally devoted to him. If Knudsen, Stettinius and Biggers had had publicity men of
their own choosing, men experienced in the propaganda of Washington, these would have fought back
and would have been of invaluable assistance to Knudsen and his associates in interpreting to them what was
happening, and guiding them through the conflict.

Knudsen and his associates were utterly defenseless.

On one occasion, Knudsen at a dinner party said wistfully: "I have learned that a gift of gab is essential in Washington."

Neither did the three men have freedom in the selection of their other OPM personnel. They won out in their choice of John Lord O'Brian, of New York, as general counsel, but then they were forced to blanket him with two young New Dealers as assistants, Milton Katz, a follower of Felix Frankfurter, and a young man classed as a Leftist who had been dismissed from the National Labor Relations Board in its drastic reorganization of late 1940. For the all-important key position of general secretary they could not have their own man, but had to take a New Dealer, Herbert Emmerich. By these and similar infiltrations active New Dealers came to saturate the OPM.

They brought conflicting philosophies on the development of the defense program within the OPM itself, which added to the conflict of philosophies between the OPM and other departments.

Biggers hastened to look into the agitation about Big Business getting the bulk of the defense business. Manifestly it was true. The Army and Navy procurement officers were used to dealing with established firms, firms which they knew were capable of carrying out contracts when they accepted them. The OPM was limited to serving in an advisory capacity. These officers were schooled in the continual conflicts of Washington. Aside from the fact that large businesses constituted going concerns ready to receive the orders, the military procurement officers had a natural reluctance against dealing with untried businesses because it added to their responsibilities. They knew that congressional committees were later to rake them over the coals in any event, but they would be in a much better position to defend themselves if they dealt with fewer firms of unquestionable national rating.

Nevertheless, Biggers went ahead and set up agencies throughout the country whereby any little man who thought he could manufacture something for the government could be assured of the necessary contact and the financing. The National Association of Manufacturers went out on a crusade to bring the little fellows in. Amazingly little came of it.

As late as mid-August Knudsen was pleading with a group of manufacturers that the defense production job be decentralized with as "little of Washington" as possible. But still wanting to avoid Washington's political or ideological controversies, he refrained from telling what the greatest drawback to Little Business was: It was not equipped to comply with the manifold government laws and regulations. For one thing, every business receiving a government contract of $10,000 or more immediately came under the Walsh-Healy labor act, by which wages of labor, hours, and working conditions were prescribed by Secretary of Labor Perkins. And to keep a careful check on the observance of this act, the New Dealers placed in the Defense Contract Service of the OPM, Peter Nehemkis, who had been active in the circles of the greatly controverted Securities and Exchange Commission. Also, Hillman's office kept a close surveillance over all contracts. Labor leaders were avowedly unenthusiastic about Little Business because it was more difficult to maintain their organization over scattered small firms.

The New Dealers charged that Biggers' setup wouldn't work because the little business man was too timid to walk into a Federal Reserve Bank. They advanced a so-called community plan whereby labor leaders, city officials and business representatives would get together in a community enterprise, to be jointly administered. There was considerable agitation about this time for joint employer-employee operation of industry, and the community proposal smacked of this and therefore frightened the employers. Biggers won the undying enmity of the New Dealers when he removed Morris L. Cooke, who was trying to set up this system, from the OPM. That Biggers did as well as anyone could in this respect, is attested by the fact that a new plan to "save little business" set up in September under Floyd B. Odlum, turned on the Government's willingness to pay as much as 15 per cent higher for defense contracts awarded to the smaller industries.

The OPM became so bewildered that its officials got to fighting among themselves. The New Dealers succeeded in splitting the Dollar-a-Year men's ranks. Batt and Biggers figuratively glared at each other. Batt, who, like Biggers, prided himself on his ability to get along with people, began agreeing with the New

Dealers about the OPM's shortcomings in an effort to make peace with them. On one occasion, at the height of the agitation, he made a public speech disparaging the OPM, in which he ranked next to Biggers. The latter reprimanded him, and the New Dealers gleefully circulated the report of the incident. They began playing Batt against Biggers and periodically circulated the report that when the OPM was reorganized, which they confidently predicted as early as the late spring, Batt might be the top defense production man. How accurate their estimate was is borne out by the fact that in the subsequent reorganization he did move up.

Donald Nelson, of Sears, Roebuck, who was to advance to the top in the melee, also sided with the New Dealers. He was in charge of procurement—for many months without any definite authority over the various procurement agencies, and also, he was subordinate to Biggers. After a clash with the latter in May, and a threat on his part to resign, the President gave him full authority over procurement, and at the same time removed him from both Knudsen's and Biggers' jurisdiction.

Whatever abilities Knudsen, Biggers, Stettinius and their aides may have had were being fairly broken by this agitation. Without any definite authority in the first place, they lost confidence in themselves. The record seems clear that Biggers, in an effort to hold the OPM together—he was the administrator next to Knudsen—became enmeshed in intrigue and he wasn't very good at it. Even Knudsen came to feel unfriendly toward him, very likely on the basis of tales that he heard. For example, Columnist Franklin's repudiated statement that Biggers looked upon Knudsen as a "naïve, honest, simple man" undoubtedly influenced Knudsen's feeling toward his deputy.

The New Dealers campaigned skillfully. They weaned Batt and Nelson away from the business ranks, leaving Knudsen, Biggers and Stettinius as the Big Three of Business. Then they divided Knudsen and Biggers.

An example of how these three men tried to avoid public controversy was their appearance before a Congressional committee in the early spring when the newspaper headlines were shouting of strikes in the defense industries and the Congressmen were seeking hungrily for support in their efforts to pass legislation dealing with the situation. Not wanting to become involved in the labor controversy, neither Knudsen, Stettinius nor Biggers would give any encouragement.

It was in this sort of atmosphere that at least 90 per cent of the country's industry came to be placed under the priority system whereby an industry to continue in business had to be graded by the OPM in the matter of essential materials it could receive, and in many instances each shipment had to be accompanied by a certificate. The priorities, in the first instance, were applied haphazardly with no definite knowledge of defense needs or of available material. They were applied by a nervous OPM, in an agitation about shortages which, at least in many instances, were more fancied than real. But when a commodity was placed under a priority, it made no difference whether the country was bulging with it, a shortage was thereby created. A shortage was created because a manufacturer, to get any of the material, had to wade through an endless stream of red tape in Washington.

Applications for priority ratings, for permits for specific shipments, lay in the countless wicker baskets of the OPM for weeks at a time. In numerous cases they were lost altogether. Subordinate Dollar-a-Year men administering particular commodities came and went in the continual agitation and confusion; clerical staffs were being frequently shaken up.

Out over the country industries were being closed down and men thrown out of work; others were being threatened with this experience—not because of the necessity of defeating Hitler, but because of confusion in Washington. This country was by way of being torn to pieces without Hitler having to fire a shot.

The confusion, the utter impotency of the OPM, can be better understood when it is realized that it was seriously maimed by the New Dealers as early as April. Although they were not to move in for the final kill until September, an earlier deft move on the part of Mr. Roosevelt left the OPM with a gaping wound in its side with which no agency could operate efficiently.

CHAPTER IV

The Henderson-Knudsen Conflict

Mr. Roosevelt, faced with a gigantic and often seemingly impossible administrative task, has frequently accomplished his immediate purposes by quietly shifting the emphasis among his alphabetical agencies, or creating new ones. Not infrequently, Washington's most alert newspapermen continue to deal with what they consider to be an authoritative agency, only to learn later that the authority has been transferred to another group.

The full implication of the President's move against the OPM in April was lost upon the newspapermen and on the country as a whole. Thus business men continued to bring their problems to the OPM, and finding a state of helplessness there, with little or no satisfaction to be found elsewhere in the confusion of Washington, returned home to add to the flooding criticism of Knudsen and his aides.

In the presidential campaign, public attention was riveted on just how and where the industrialists would fit into the defense program. Thus, when Knudsen, Stettinius and their associates were placed on the National Defense Advisory Commission (NDAC), in May 1940, the debate proceeded on the lines of whether this was an authoritative body. It sounded formidable enough.

Little or no attention was paid to the setting up, about the same time, of the OEM (Office of Emergency Management). It was placed in charge of a member of the President's secretariat, W. H. McReynolds, an elderly government career man and an expert on personnel. Therefore, it seemed to be nothing more than an unobtrusive agency to handle personnel and routine. Indeed, under McReynolds that is what it was.

Then, when the President on January 7, 1941, responded to the agitation for a central and authoritative defense production head by establishing the OPM under the dual control of Knudsen and Hillman, it was not generally noticed that it was placed under OEM. The debate, editorial and political, turned on the question of whether such a two-headed animal could function effectively. If it had the effect of quieting or misleading those who were demanding that industrialists and not New Dealers be given the defense production job, it also confirmed the worst suspicions of the New Dealers that they were being given the runaround. Henderson was not placed in this new setup. This was when he left town in a huff, and when the New Dealers let go their attack against the Dollar-a-Year men.

[48]

In the bitterness that followed on the part of the New Dealers, and the bewilderment on the part of the Dollar-a-Year men, it is doubtful if the latter realized just when and how the New Dealers returned to the picture.

Three quiet moves by Mr. Roosevelt, only one of which attracted much attention and none of which was considered related to the other, affected it.

When the President sent the $7,000,000,000 lend-lease bill to Congress in March, Congressman John Taber, of New York, Republican member of the House Appropriations Committee, told Speaker Sam Rayburn that if Harry Hopkins was going to administer the fund there would be difficulty in getting it approved by the House. Rayburn agreed and asked Mr. Roosevelt about it. Apparently misunderstanding his conversation with the President he returned to the Capitol and assured members of the House that Hopkins was to have nothing to do with the seven-billion-dollar spending. Then when the bill was passed, the President quietly made known that Hopkins was to administer the program and would continue to live at the White House.

On April 11, a new price-control agency with Henderson as director was announced—OPACS (Office of Price Administration and Civilian Supply). On April 23, Wayne Coy, one of the President's "anonymous" aides, a 38-year-old ace of the New Dealers, relieved McReynolds as head of the OEM. Under Coy the OEM ceased to be simply an agency handling personnel and routine matters.

It became the directive force under Hopkins of the defense program.

Coy was a protégé of Paul McNutt, coming up in Indiana politics under him. McNutt took him to the Philippines as his secretary and brought him to Washington when he, McNutt, became Federal Security Administrator. Through McNutt's influence Coy served as state WPA administrator of Indiana under Hopkins, and came to be an associate of the latter.

Knudsen and his aides were, by the President's order, made subordinate to Coy; he passed upon their policies and supplied their personnel—this young man whose only non-political job had been that of publishing a weekly newspaper in Indiana.

Henderson, also operating under the Hopkins-Coy liaison, promptly set out to build up an organization which in a few months would have 1,400 professors and economists, together with their clerical help, to have an annual appropriation of nearly $4,000,000, and to be the most all-powerful of the defense agencies, completely overwhelming the OPM.

Hopkins, who when he landed in England the first time, spoke emotionally of how the son of an Iowa blacksmith had risen to the estate of associating with Kings and Queens and such a world leader as Winston Churchill, tactfully had nothing to say now that he had become America's second most important man of the Second

World War. Suffering from a stomach ailment so badly that he frequently had to leave the dinner table —more often he ate in his private quarters—this man who came up as a social worker to spend millions for the New Deal, was now in charge of spending the super billions of the defense program!

More than any other one man he caught the spirit of Mr. Roosevelt's New Deal at the outset and gave it practical application by blending reform with relief in the vast expenditures which he directed as WPA administrator. A Senate committee in 1938 revealed that he used relief money against political opponents of the President. As he sat before this committee of aroused Senators—more aroused because he had used relief money to attempt to defeat some of their colleagues— he appeared to be in such failing health that it was not thought he could live more than a few months. He told the Senators frankly that he would do anything the President wanted him to do. So they dismissed him and fell in with the plan to take him from the WPA and make him Secretary of Commerce where he wouldn't have relief money to spend.

In his more than six years of spending, the National Debt had risen to nearly forty-five billions. He had used relief funds to advance the organization of the CIO against the American Federation of Labor, the CIO having been conceived by the New Dealers as a socio-political accompaniment of their Social Revolution. Instance after instance developed of his having informed state WPA administrators that there would be a CIO-engineered strike in their community on a certain date and he wanted the strikers to be immediately certified for relief.

' As his health grew worse in the Department of Commerce, the President brought him to the White House to live and sought to breathe new life into him. Some of the inherited-wealth men in and around the New Deal arranged an endowment for him by which he could live comfortably with his motherless daughter by his second wife and continue to pay alimony to his first wife and their three children.

Had Mr. Roosevelt proclaimed the new defense setup, undoubtedly it would have created a storm of criticism from his political opponents throughout the country. Under it the confusion was to become intensified because Hopkins, whom youngish Wayne Coy had to consult, was out of the country a good part of the time. He made a second trip to London. He went to Moscow. Coy had access to the President, but because of the pressure of the latter's work, problems lay on his desk for weeks at a time. Coy could not make a major decision without consulting with the President or Hopkins.

In this loose arrangement, Henderson, with his new authority and his natural aggressiveness, spread out his activities. He once said:

"I think it is a paradox that someone who believes in laissez faire more than most anybody else in the administration should be the price administrator."

Until he gained Mr. Roosevelt's favor and particularly that of Harry Hopkins, by giving them a political explanation of the 1937 so-called recession, Henderson had not been one of the top New Dealers. While working for the Russell Sage Foundation in 1933 he appeared as a consumers' representative at one of the open forums Hugh Johnson, then generalissimo of the NRA, was holding. He annoyed Johnson so much with his aggressiveness that Johnson finally suggested sarcastically that he stick around Washington for awhile to see what it was all about. Henderson did, and landed a job in the NRA, subsequently becoming head of its rather vaguely defined Research and Planning Division. When the NRA folded up he was sort of on the New Deal hands and working at odd jobs, until after he gained the favor of the President and Hopkins and landed the job in 1938 of executive secretary of the Senate Monopoly or Temporary National Economic Committee. The following year he was made a member of the Securities and Exchange Commission and from that time he was a vigorous voice in the New Deal.

Henderson was not essentially a reformer, and unlike many of his associates had never posed as an Intellectual. He didn't call himself Doctor or Professor, and he preferred the term "interpretative statistician" to that of economist in describing his profession. He worked his way through school by tending to people's babies and their lawns, by playing semi-pro baseball and football. Whereas his associates had been portrayed and had portrayed themselves as Mind over Matter, he was distinctly Mind *and* Matter, and liked to brag about the fist fights he had been in. Business men did not associate him with the "Theorists" or the "Brilliants." They rather welcomed his selection as price czar because he unmistakably had the figures on a business or industry when he advanced against it.

The Dollar-a-Year men warmed right up to him when they arrived in Washington. They didn't understand either the language or the baleful glances of Henderson's associates. But there was nothing antagonistic in his reception of them. He didn't look upon them as something suspect simply because they were industrialists. His young followers took part; in fact, were ringleaders in the campaign against the Dollar-a-Year men, but he got around and cultivated them, and the word went around town that he got along splendidly with Knudsen, with Batt, with Donald Nelson, and Biggers, and so on. He never confounded the Dollar-a-Year men by talking about "Social Justice" and other such abstract subjects. He spoke altogether in terms of production as if he were just a fellow industrialist. Admittedly one of the ablest of the New Dealers, it caused considerable excitement in New Deal ranks when he was left out of the OPM setup when it was created in January. His treatment seemed to leave no doubt that the Business Men were to handle the defense production job.

But when he went away, boiling over with indignation, he kept a close watch for Hopkins' departure from London for home. Thus it happened that when

Hopkins arrived at Bermuda, Henderson was there waiting for him. Then and there he convinced Hopkins of the necessity for a price controller and, a man who a short while before had been out of the defense picture, bounded back into it on both feet and with fists figuratively flying.

His over-all job was to prevent inflation. This bore on just about every endeavor in this country. It gave him a voice in the granting of priorities for defense materials, and in his capacity as administrator of consumer supplies, he had control over the allocation of materials left over for consumer industries. He had a voice in the profits which an industry made, over the wages it paid; in the nation's tax bill; in the general credit structure; in the price which farmers received for their crops. He did not have authority in all these matters, and it was to be seen how effective would be his voice, but a voice in something on his part was compelling because he was not a blushing violet.

On July 18, he announced that automobile production had to be cut by 50 per cent without so much as consulting with Knudsen or the OPM. Knudsen and the automobile manufacturers had previously agreed upon a 20 per cent cut, and they were in the course of discussing a further reduction to be planned so as not to bring about great unemployment.

Henderson learned that Knudsen had asked the automobile manufacturers to confer with him on a particular day. He promptly called them in on the day before. For the first time Knudsen showed anger. He announced that the OPM would pass on the question of when and how much automobile reduction would be ordered. Henderson grinned confidently. During this set-to it developed that Mr. Roosevelt had had on his desk for several weeks two separate orders defining Henderson's scope and that of OPM, one prepared by Henderson and one by the OPM. Both sides waited confidently for Mr. Roosevelt's word. Instead, he went off to sea in early August for a historic meeting with Winston Churchill.

Then on August 11, when a good part of the world must have been speculating on the President's whereabouts, when the White House professed to have no information about him, and the State Department, Army and Navy professed to be in the dark, Marriner S. Eccles, governor of the Federal Reserve Board, produced a decree signed by the President authorizing the board to take over the control of installment credit in the country.

It was of tremendous importance to the lives of the American people, but of immediate concern to Knudsen was the fact that the question of automobile production was now in the hands of Eccles, collaborating with Henderson. They could say what was to be the extent of the reduction and when, by simply shortening the term of installment payments.

The decree was said to be necessary to curb inflation, and the country's editors were generally agreed that we must not have inflation. But it so happened that the country's installment credit system was one of the earlier aversions of the New Dealers. It is difficult to think of any one thing that has had a more profound effect on the lives of people in this country than the institution of installment credit. Under it, people of lower incomes have been able to purchase automobiles, radios, sewing machines, electric refrigerators, furniture and countless other necessities and luxuries of life. The system had many critics, but it was nevertheless definitely woven into our economic fabric, and it was substantial enough to weather the 1929 collapse. It would be a tremendous undertaking to describe its full scope—the numbers of men and women to whom it gave a livelihood. The thousands and thousands of little "second-rate" furniture and clothing stores were scarcely more than a speck on the whole picture. Railroads and steamship lines had even come to selling tickets on the installment plan.

Mr. Roosevelt publicly expostulated against the automobile phase of it in 1937. He attributed as one of the causes of the "recession" of that year, the action of the automobile manufacturers in extending the installment period. The government on the eve of the presidential campaign the year before had given two billion dollars to the veterans in payment of their bonus. The automobile manufacturers, through extension of the installment period and high-pressure campaigns, had gobbled most of it up, Mr. Roosevelt complained.

Early in 1941, Eccles, having been pushed more and more out of the Washington bureaucratic picture in a feud with Secretary of the Treasury Henry Morgenthau, hit upon the control of installment credit as a function for himself. Morgenthau opposed him over the following months. Finally, from out on the high seas somewhere, came an order which excluded the government agencies such as the Federal Housing Administration and its Farm and Home Agency, which sold many household appliances on the easy payment plan, but brought all private installment credit in the country under the control of Eccles. He and Henderson worked well together.

Was it necessary to pull the country back from the brink of inflation? The OPM and Henderson were announcing that the public was going to get lessening numbers of automobiles, electric refrigerators, washing machines, radios and the like, anyhow.

Regardless of its necessity, the order, the authority for which Mr. Roosevelt said was given him in congressional acts of 1917 and 1933, originated in the New Dealers' desire to control this tremendous phase of American life!

And it was applied at the height of confusion over the defense program, which necessarily added to the confusion. The respective scope of Knudsen's and Henderson's authority was not defined. Instead, a lever was given to Eccles and Henderson, working together, against Knudsen.

The agitation against the OPM had a way of recurring in waves, in so far as its public manifestation was concerned. There was never a day from a few weeks after the end of the presidential campaign that it enjoyed a smooth-running, orderly organization, but after its fairly complete demoralization in mid-April and the subsequent haphazard application of priorities reached down to the roots of American industry, there followed intermittent surges of public complaint. These were accompanied by demands that the President set up one over-all defense production administrator. This agitation, as reflected in the newspapers, in outbursts from Congress, and in the excitement of the Washington newspaper corps, would run for three or four days and then the OPM would enjoy a respite of a week or ten days.

But by mid-August the general opinion of the Washington newspapermen was that Mr. Roosevelt would be forced "to do something." The evidence was that he fought hard against "doing sonmething." Up until the time he left for his meeting with Winston Churchill there was no indication that he intended to give in to the agitation.

Throughout the summer, Bernard M. Baruch, who served as an over-all defense production administrator in the First World War, was a frequent guest of Mr. Roosevelt's, and reports would circulate that he was to have the job again, which he dearly wanted. The fact is that newspapermen who accompanied Mr. Roosevelt to Warm Springs, Georgia, in the interim between his election and inauguration in the winter of 1932–33, were startled by the hostility of his entourage toward the famous financier. Those who were in a position to know the new President's mind said there was one thing the newspapermen could depend upon, and that was, that Baruch would never serve in Mr. Roosevelt's administration. Baruch had opposed Mr. Roosevelt in the pre-convention campaign.

On one occasion, the newspapermen ran into Baruch at the hotel and asked what had brought him to Warm Springs. He explained that he had been at his winter place in South Carolina and had returned North and Mr. Roosevelt had asked him to come back to Warm Springs. That afternoon, when the newspapermen went to Mr. Roosevelt's press conference in his cottage, Baruch was present. They asked Mr. Roosevelt if he could give any information on Baruch's visit.

Mr. Roosevelt looked straight at Baruch and said:

"Why, Bernie was over at his place in South Carolina and asked if he might drop by. That's all there is to it."

Baruch grinned sheepishly.

But in early August, Judge Sam Rosenman of the New York State Supreme Court arrived in Washington on a rather mysterious mission of straightening out Mr. Roosevelt's administrative difficulties. There was to be a complete hiatus in the functioning of the organizations likely to be affected while he moved around. The rumor persisted all over gossipy Washington that he was to effect the long-waited over-all defense production organization. When Mr. Roosevelt went to Albany as governor, Rosenman was a government employee in charge of the legislative drafting service. Mr. Roosevelt named him counsel to the governor and subsequently appointed him to the State Supreme Court. From his earlier acquaintance with the President, he was to be one of his most intimate friends. He frequently advised the President on policies and helped in the drafting of his more important speeches.

Because of his known influence with the President, Rosenman's comings and goings around Washington, his conferences with this official and that, were closely watched—over a period of three weeks.

When Mr. Roosevelt returned from his meeting with Churchill he seemed to resent the suggestion that Rosenman was working out the over-all defense job. Rosenman's activities, the President insisted, were confined to straightening out the conflict in priority administration between the OPM and Henderson's OPACS. This conflict had been in evidence for more than three months and smoldering before that.

Mr. Roosevelt told inquirers rather curtly that Rosenman's work was confined to ironing out this conflict; and that otherwise the functioning of his hodge-podge defense setup was satisfactory to him.

But out of a clear sky, on August 28, he announced the creation of another alphabetical agency to ride atop of all the other defense alphabetical agencies, except the OEM, which was the directive agency under him. The new agency was named Supply Priorities and Allocations Board, the SPAB. Vice-President Henry A. Wallace was placed at the head.

At the White House it was explained that this was not yet the "real thing" by way of an over-all production organization, but that it might easily move into that position. The process of watching it "move" was to be the pastime of Washington in the following weeks.

One thing it did immediately, however, was to mark the New Dealers' final victory against Knudsen, Stettinius and Biggers, as well as to reward the enterprise of Batt and Donald Nelson in having sided with the former. Biggers, who had been serving, so far as appearances were concerned, in second place in the defense production structure, just under Knudsen, was assigned as "minister" to London, a position without statutory standing, and even in this capacity he was to serve under Averell Harriman, who was moved up as "Co-ordinator" of lend-lease supplies in both Britain and Russia. Biggers' new assignment was what, in the language of Washington backbiting and confusion, is described as "getting a man out of town." Batt, with whom he had fought in the OPM, and who was subordinate to him, was sent on a mission to Russia.

But Nelson was to get the biggest "plum" of all. The explanation accompanying the announcement of the new alphabetical agency was that Wallace likely wouldn't have too much time to devote to it and that Nelson would serve as executive director in his place. When the priorities conflict between Henderson and the OPM broke out, the New Dealers constantly advanced Nelson for Biggers' place, Stettinius' place, or even Knudsen's, "because he could get along with Henderson."

Knudsen was still to retain his place as co-director of OPM, and in this capacity he had a place on the SPAB. But except for show purposes he had been completely subordinated in the defense picture. The main thing which official Washington was quick to note was that the New Dealers had a majority of the board, four out of the seven members. The board was unquestionably to be dominated by Henderson, with Nelson a co-dominator as long as he co-operated with Henderson. In the realignment Mr. Roosevelt took note of the frequent criticism against the Office of Price Administration and Civilian Supplies, OPACS having both jurisdiction over prices and allocation of civilian supplies left over after defense needs had been satisfied. So he cut the OPACS down to OPA, Office of Price Administration, and put the CS, Civilian Supplies administration, in the OPM. The criticism against this dual administration had arisen out of Henderson's conflict with Knudsen. So Mr. Roosevelt acted on it. He split the alphabetical array in two and kept Henderson in charge of both parts!

And at one of the earliest meetings of SPAB, in mid-September, it was agreed to let Henderson determine how much automobile production should be curtailed. He forthwith announced a 48 per cent reduction, and thus after some five months of behind-the-scenes and open conflict in Washington, the thousands of men dependent for their livelihoods upon the many phases of the automobile industry knew what was to be done. For a long time they had been suspect to the butcher, the baker and the candlestick maker. Undoubtedly they had gone home many a night during this period, and after getting the children to bed, discussed with their wives what the future had in store for them. Finally, they were at least to have some light, and in that way of men when pressed to the wall, probably find some way out.

The whole Knudsen-Henderson episode well illustrated the fact that the defense production program was being administered in a continuation of the ideological conflict between Leftists and Rightists which has prevailed in this country for eight years and which has engulfed a large part of the world. Weaving in and out of the months-long controversy was the so-called "social consciousness" crusade, which, if it was not actually running counter to this country's defense efforts, was at least running parallel to them.

Knudsen and Henderson were scarcely more than spokesmen for the two sides. Behind the latter were hundreds of theoretical men—professors, economists, sociologists—who insisted that as administrator of consumer supplies he should have jurisdiction over the automobile industry. Knudsen's aides—practical business men—contended that an industry so closely linked with national defense should come under OPM.

Fundamentally, there was little or no difference between Knudsen and Henderson as to the end to be attained. Although the public is likely to recall Knudsen as having called for a 20 per cent cut and Henderson for 50 and 48 per cent cuts, finally announcing the latter when the industry was placed under his jurisdiction, this was because he had a better aptitude for hitting the headlines than Knudsen. As applied over a period and in different industries as the 48 per cent figure was to be, the net result was to be only slightly different from the end Knudsen was seeking sans publicity.

Far more significant than the conflict over jurisdiction between Knudsen and Henderson was the steady propaganda against the automobile industry which accompanied it and with which Henderson himself had nothing to do. Against Knudsen, personally, it was to the effect that he was protecting the automobile industry. Leftist publications printed such statements as that, while he himself was patriotic, his will-power wilted when he was in the presence of Alfred P. Sloan, chairman of the board of General Motors.

Against the industry it was to the effect that it was traitorously using up defense metals to fill its dividend coffers. The conflict, however, really applied not at all to production for the automobile year ending in August, but to the 1942 year beginning then. Nevertheless, there were those who contended that the industry used up a vast supply of metals in its unusual production for 1941; that had it not done so, these metals would constitute a defense reservoir. Representatives of the industry claimed, on the other hand, that had not its increased production pressed the steel, aluminum, copper and other metal industries, they would not have attained the production capacity which they did. And this seems just as logical as the frequent statement that Mr. Roosevelt should be thanked for letting the British and French get aircraft in this country right after the outbreak of the war because their orders made it possible for our aircraft industry to expand its production.

The propaganda campaign was carried on against the automobile industry in the widespread misconception and representation that it can be wholly switched over to defense production. The most optimistic estimates on the part of the industry are that not more than 15 per cent of its facilities can be used in defense production. On the other hand, it was estimated that half of the workers would be thrown out of employment by the reduced automobile production, and of these a half would not be absorbed in defense production.

Significant of the atmosphere in which the country was proceeding was the fact that a lot of agitation against the industry was being stirred up by the leaders of the automobile workers' union with whom the whole industry was dealing presumably in a spirit of goodwill and fair play. The union had won its fight against the industry, contracts had been negotiated. Just what was the purpose of the further agitation?

Typical of this agitation was the appearance in Washington in the spring of several union leaders headed by Walter Reuther. He contended that the industry was not making use of all its available "space."

By utilizing this space, he said, the industry could build 500 planes a day. Planes, of course, are not made out of "space"; "space" does not constitute an idle plant facility. The New Dealers, themselves, dismissed the so-called plan, but for several months afterwards defense officials were being badgered by reporters for Leftist publications with the question:

"Do you intend to make use of the Reuther plan?"

Philip Murray, head of the CIO, had a similar plan for the steel industry.

It was yet to be shown that the steel and automobile executives were not anxious to make money. The auto industry was taking defense contracts just as fast as it could get them, and just as rapidly it was tooling up to carry them out. The workers were the ones to be hit in the readjustments, not the executives or the investors. As of the end of June the industry had been given defense orders for only two and a half billion dollars to extend through 1943. Its annual automobile business is from three and a half to five billions.

Stettinius, who was weary of the Washington struggle but wanted to remain in the defense picture, was assigned to assisting Hopkins in the administration of lend-lease supplies. No longer was he to have to sign priority orders which he had not formulated, striking at American industry.

On the night of the shift, he visited Washington's Translux Theater with Mrs. Stettinius. When they had become comfortably seated she remarked:

"I told you to stay with U. S. Steel."

One of the first things that Nelson was to find out was that the priorities division under Stettinius had been one scarcely more than a name. Once a material was placed under a priority then army and navy officers could use the preferred ratings given those agencies indiscriminately. It really did a manufacturer of non-defense material no good to have a rating, because the Government procurement agencies had higher ratings. The OPM had no way of checking these agencies or of making them prove their needs. On one day, in one particular order, the army bought 39½ million yards of khaki cotton uniform twill, at a cost of $23,334,000. This was estimated to be enough for 10,000,000 uniforms. And this was just one order. Notwithstanding that our army was being motorized, the army in one order contracted for 61,000 halters and $450,000 worth of new saddles. Another such order called for 1,500,-000 thermometers.

A widely circulated story in the First World War was the practice of each army officer to add 10 per cent to the estimates for material as they passed over his desk. This sort of buying would create a shortage of anything, anywhere. Baruch got the authority in the First World War to make the army and navy prove their estimates of needs.

Nelson set out to get this authority in his OPM priorities division. In an effort to bring some order out of the chaos, he also sought to have the priority system switched to a system of allocations based upon real needs for the military services and for the country's non-defense industry. He had not been successful as late as mid-September, but he was a very strong-minded man.

Nelson, undoubtedly a capable man and, because of his thirty years' experience with the more or less paternalistic policies of Sears, Roebuck, not as alarmed by the New Dealers as his business associates, found the applications for priorities from harassed industries three weeks deep when he took over the priorities division. The SPAB decided, after all the agitation about shortages and defense needs, that one of its first undertakings should be to find out what the actual situation was!

The key to the constant shuffling and reshuffling of the alphabetical agencies was given in Mr. Roosevelt's emphatic statement that the new agency, the SPAB, was to be subordinate to him. Mr. Roosevelt was determined to retain direct control over the defense spending. It was his very definite conviction that the agitation for an over-all defense production administrator, clothed with full authority, grew out of efforts to get the spending program away from him, and his associate New Dealers were just as convinced as he that this was the game.

So, come what may in the future by way of agitation against the defense setup, there was no question but that, if and when Mr. Roosevelt should be forced to bow to it, his action would be no more than the shuffling of alphabetical agencies and the creation of new ones.

And whatever future picture might be presented, the real setup in Washington was likely to be: Henderson to Hopkins to Roosevelt. HHR was the real agency.

The British Leftist economist, Harold Laski, visited Washington during Mr. Roosevelt's second administration. He made a profound impression on the New Dealers when he told them they had been very foolish in conducting their revolution by antagonizing Business. The thing to do, he argued, was to take Business into camp by giving it money as well as the underprivileged. They would find Business an easy tool in this way, he said, and ultimately the size of the national debt would bring about what he believed the New Dealers wanted—complete control of the credit structure and socialism.

The manner in which business men fought to get war contracts in Washington in 1941; the manner in which conservative members of Congress joined in the war of the New Dealers against Dollar-a-Year men because their districts were not getting as much of the defense billions as their due; the manner in which some of the industrialists and business men assisted the New Dealers in this fight by claiming competitors were getting more business than they, by joining in the chorus of abuse against the OPM, and the manner in which the Dollar-a-Year men fought among themselves, suggest that Laski was not talking in ignorance.

CHAPTER V

Battle of the Economists

Over the course of time many men have come to Washington seeking their place in the headlines of the day—John Randolph, of Virginia; Daniel Webster, Borah of Idaho, Dr. Townsend, Huey Long, and even Mr. Smith of the movies. For the prominence he attained in a short while, Gano Dunn should have felt proud, but he probably didn't.

Throughout the summer people in Washington were to refer to the "Gano Dunn report" as they might speak of the Battle of Yorktown, the Hawley-Smoot tariff bill, the Bonus Marchers—as if it were something everybody, of course, knew about. It was, in fact, the report which, along with a similar report on aluminum needs, was to break the OPM's back and place the New Dealers in the saddle.

Mr. Dunn himself was an executive of the White Engineering Company. He was one of the country's outstanding construction engineers. At one time he was reputed to be one of eleven men in the world to understand the Einstein theory. He prepared a report early in the year estimating the amount of steel the country would need in its undertaking of crushing Hitler. The New Dealers were just waiting for a Dollar-a-Year man to open his mouth. Their economists got busy, and in a few weeks had prepared exhaustive studies to show that Dunn had fallen short by some 10,000,000 tons annually.

There were, roughly, some 5,000 economists in Washington. Practically every government agency had some, and in turn the various bureaus within the agency had others. The popular song, "It's a Great Day for the Irish," gave way in Washington shortly after the advent of the New Deal to "It's a Great Day for the Economists."

One might believe, from the agitation of the economists, that they must have been a downtrodden race. They had, over the period of recent history, been griping that their bosses took the figures they prepared and made ponderous and attention-attracting statements with them. The economists themselves considered they were underpaid and received no recognition. Some very few, such as Dr. Roger Babson and Dr. Irving Fisher, both of whom predicted the 1929 prosperity would never come to an end, developed the knack of selling their figures on a syndicate basis and attained national recognition.

By and large, however, the economists were a restless lot, and such people are bound to attain expression sooner or later. They did with the New Deal.

Many of the New Deal economists used their theses

as springboards to high administrative position: for example, Leon Henderson. All the rest with a grain of ambition in their systems were striving daily to do the same. Isador Lubin, in the Department of Labor, attained national recognition and influence in the New Deal with his statistics on unemployment; in the Department of Agriculture, Mordecai Ezekiel attracted attention with a thesis that every family should have a minimum income of $2,500 a year; others impressed their identities on hurly-burly Washington with theses showing that monopolies were responsible for America's economic ills. Those who prepared the thesis against Gano Dunn's estimate of steel needs became immortalized in New Deal circles.

On the basis of it, the New Dealers established in the American mind the phrase "Business as usual" to describe the Dollar-a-Year men. They were, according to the New Dealers, men so traitorous that rather than turn from "Business as usual" and build new plants for fear of having too many plants at war's end, they would let Hitler with his funny little mustache come right over to our shores.

On the other hand, the Dollar-a-Year men dubbed the New Dealers a "Business as usual" crowd because of their insistence upon maintaining and furthering their "labor gains," and also for their insistence upon carrying out, on top of the defense program, their social building projects. But the Dollar-a-Year men did not have the propaganda facilities that the New Dealers had, and the result was that every time they uttered the "Business as usual" slogan they only further marked themselves in that category.

The whole controversy had little fundamental relation to the defeat of Hitler, yet this was the vehicle which the New Dealers used. It dealt primarily with the economy of this country.

At the turn of the year the predominant school of New Dealers was advocating—or rather just acting on—the assumption that this country's productive capacity was to be stepped up to the highest pitch imaginable, regardless of defense needs or the ability of people in this country to buy. It was to be a production of plenty in a country of plenty, so that all the people would share in its great wealth. It was a far cry from the policy of scarcity which had been pursued in agriculture, but it came from that school which has long held that progress is held up by the restriction of production on the part of big business and monopolies.

A party to this agitation—indeed, one of its ringleaders—was the advanced "liberal" British economist, John Maynard Keynes. He had already had a tremendous influence on this country's economy with his monetary and government-spending theories, which he could not get accepted at home, but for which he found a fertile field in the early New Deal. An associate of the New Dealers, and operating among them, although ostensibly present as a member of a British war commission, he argued that "needs" should not be considered; that American industry should be stepped up to its highest productive capacity to determine just what the capacity really could be.

In answer to the business men's query as to what would become of the idle plants after the war, the New Dealers argued that they could be maintained by the government as stand-bys. The business men were convinced that the New Dealers intended to use the additional plants for competition, and they were seemingly justified in this conviction from what happened in the aluminum industry.

Henderson was a party to the agitation to the extent of insisting that with wage earners having more money to spend there had to be an increased supply of consumers' goods in order to prevent exorbitant price rises. At the height of the agitation, Secretary of the Treasury Henry Morgenthau stepped in to say that he had other plans for the increased earnings of workers. He planned to siphon them off in taxes and savings.

It was typical of the confusion that so many voices were agitating conflicting policies of tremendous bearing on the lives of the American people in a time of national emergency. Mr. Roosevelt let the agitation go right along as something of only academic concern. But businesses were being wrecked and threatened throughout the country because of it.

It was into this sort of agitation that Dunn stepped with his report, or rather two reports, on steel needs and steel supplies. His conclusion was that no additional steel plants were needed. During the investigation in 1938 by the so-called Senate Monopoly Committee, or TNEC (Temporary National Economic Committee), of which Henderson was the guiding spirit, the steel industry was bitterly denounced by the New Dealers for continuing to carry run-down and surplus plants. Maintenance of these plants, the New Dealers contended, was charged to the cost of steel. Now, these plants had been revived, and the New Dealers wanted additional ones.

The cyclonic attack against Dunn, based on the counter estimates worked out by New Deal economists, particularly Stacy May and Melvin G. de Chazeau, forced him to resign. May, a member of the OPM, for the past eight years had been assistant director of social sciences for the Rockefeller Foundation. Unlike Dunn, he had never built anything but figures. Along with Dunn, although this did not attract so much attention, C. W. Kellogg, head of the Edison Electric Institute, a trade organization of power utilities, was also forced to resign. The New Dealers charged that he grossly underestimated aluminum needs.

It is not really important, except to the vanity of the economists concerned, what the respective estimates were. Nobody had any definite basis of needs. And the business men certainly seemed logical when they contended that had the New Dealers been listened to, this country would have devoted two years pretty much to extending its production capacity rather than to producing against Hitler.

Even May estimated that to increase plant capacity sufficient to produce 10,000,000 additional tons of steel annually would have in itself required 2,000,000 tons of steel. And assuming that every inch of a battleship is steel, which, of course, is not the case, 2,000,000 tons would be enough to build fifty-seven battleships of the *North Carolina* type.

What would seem to be more important is that this agitation was used by the New Dealers to get control of the defense program, and that they succeeded in doing so. In mid-July, it had Knudsen and his aides so unnerved that, to meet it, they periodically announced plans for steel and aluminum expansions. This amounted to an admission that they had been wrong in the first instance, and only gave the New Dealers further agitating material.

But it is significant that, as of late September, no serious steps had been taken appreciably to increase steel plant facilities, except the expansions which the industry had undertaken outside the controversy. The agitation was continuing, however, and the New Dealers were now applying the "heat" to Jesse Jones, charging his Reconstruction Finance Corporation was a bottleneck. Jones was not easily stampeded. Plans had been made to step up aluminum production by 870 million pounds annually at some time many months in the future.

It is rather a sad commentary on men in whom people have placed their trust that the agitation about aluminum and steel had even other motives than the New Dealers' desire to get control of the defense program. It had ramifications which Knudsen, with his non-political mind, could not possibly have comprehended.

It was a prolongation, in the guise of national defense, of the New Dealers' war on the steel industry, "Old Andy" Mellon's Aluminum Company, and the private power industry.

These three industries—steel, aluminum, and power —had been on the New Dealers' list of "something to be done about" ever since they assumed control of the government. These industries play an important part in American life. In the case of steel, all modern living turns around it—the automobile industry, housing, railroads, and so on without end. Also, steel, looking for more abundant and, collaterally, cheaper labor, was at the forefront in encouraging the tremendous immigration from Southern and Eastern Europe which began around the turn of the century and continued in full force until checked by immigration laws in the latter twenties. The immigrants of this period were to have much to do with the political complexion of this country and to form a substantial nucleus for the New Deal.

Early in the New Deal a group of industrialists were in to see Mr. Roosevelt and wish him godspeed. As the group prepared to leave, a representative of Eugene Grace, president of Bethlehem Steel Corporation, hung back, and said:

"Mr. President: Mr. Grace asked that I extend his best wishes."

"Oh, yes," replied Mr. Roosevelt, "tell Gene he'll never make another million dollars."

In the roaring twenties, Mr. Grace had made $1,000,000 a year in salary and bonuses.

In 1937, the New Dealers were hard put to explain the so-called recession. Leon Henderson produced the explanation that the steel companies were responsible because they maintained fixed prices and held up building, and from then on Henderson was in Mr. Roosevelt's favor. A blistering New Deal attack on the steel companies followed.

Early in 1941, Mellon's gift to the nation, one of the greatest art galleries in the world, the building of which alone cost $13,000,000, was opened in Washington. Mr. Roosevelt dedicated it. Not once did he mention Mellon's name. His Aluminum Company had long been held by politicians, even before the New Deal, to be a monopoly.

From the time Bob Jackson, then solicitor in the Treasury, tried to put the old man in jail in 1934 for alleged criminal evasion of taxes, the New Deal had kept up a steady attack on the Aluminum Company.

By hammering away at the Aluminum Company over a period of months, by charging that it was deliberately hampering national defense, by charging that it had agreements with the Germans, the New Dealers encouraged the Reconstruction Finance Corporation

[79]

to set up two rivals in the aluminum production business, Reynolds Metal Products of Richmond, Virginia, whose head was a heavy contributor to the New Dealers in the 1940 campaign, and the Bohn Brass and Metals Company on the Pacific coast.

As soon as the RFC agreed to finance Reynolds, three New Dealers left to accept high-pay jobs with the firm. One was an attorney in the Department of Justice who had prepared a recent anti-trust complaint against the Aluminum Company.

But, what is more, the attack also influenced the RFC to finance Henry J. Kaiser, prominent builder and promoter, to the extent of $9,000,000 to develop magnesium on the Pacific coast. Magnesium can be used for many purposes as a substitute for aluminum.

Tommy Corcoran represented Kaiser in this transaction. His fee is variously estimated to have been all the way from $60,000 to $200,000. Tommy's operations of this sort during the first six months of the year were generally reputed in Washington to have netted him well over a half million dollars. Kaiser with his associates in shipbuilding and dredging enterprises had contracts with the government totaling around $800,000,000. Although Corcoran was out of the government, he still had the run of the departments, many of whose lawyers owed their jobs to him. The fact that his activities were permitted added to the distrust and suspicion of Washington.

Ickes was the driving force behind the attack on the Aluminum Company. Aside from the fact that it constituted one of his pet aversions, it furnished him with a vehicle in his campaign for public ownership of power plants, to be administered by his department. Aluminum manufacture is closely related to power production. The subject of public or private ownership of power plants has been a political issue in this country for at least twenty-five years, an issue in many municipalities even longer than that. Ickes, in the first eight years of the New Deal, had gone a long way toward accomplishing public ownership through the simple device of pouring out millions of dollars of public works funds enabling municipalities either to buy private plants or to set up plants in competition to them.

These public works funds had been appropriated by Congress to create employment.

Ickes climaxed his attack on the Aluminum Company with a statement in June that "when the war against Hitler is lost, if it is lost, the Aluminum Company can be held responsible." And he was upheld by the New Dealish Truman committee. As an example of how this committee operated, it had Grenville Holden, a Dollar-a-Year OPM consultant on aluminum and magnesium, before it for several days. The committee established to its satisfaction that the Aluminum Company is a monopoly, not because of any patents it may have on manufacture, but because it controls all the available high-grade bauxite deposits from which aluminum is made—in Arkansas and in British and Dutch Guiana. It seems there is an abundance of low-grade bauxite and a similar deposit, in this country and elsewhere, but that for aluminum purposes it is commercially unprofitable.

After having established this, the committee pressed the hapless Mr. Holden with why, when men came to him with proposals to manufacture aluminum from low-grade deposits in Utah, Arkansas, elsewhere, he would give them no encouragement. Was he trying to protect the Aluminum Company from competition? Either the Aluminum Company is a monopoly because it owns all the commercially profitable bauxite deposits, or it isn't. If it is, then it should not be hard to understand why a man in OPM charged with getting aluminum for defense purposes, would want to deal with the Aluminum Company, and not be interested in some man who after all these years believed he could produce aluminum from the low-grade deposits!

It was the New Dealers' contention that had the Aluminum Company not exercised a monopoly and held down production all these years, the country would now be wallowing in aluminum and could build so many planes as to smother Hitler utterly. Which is undoubtedly true if it were also wallowing in the other necessary materials, the aviation plants, the skilled workers and pilots, the guns and the thousand and one other essentials of air warfare.

This is not intended as any defense of the Aluminum Company. It is related for the purpose of throwing a little light into the contentious atmosphere in which this country's defense program was being carried out, an atmosphere that was bidding fair to demoralize a large segment of American life at a time when unity was the need.

A subcommittee of the House Military Affairs committee, headed by Representative Charles I. Faddis of Pennsylvania, a Democrat, had been investigating the situation. It developed not only that the Aluminum Company had greatly expanded its facilities with its own money, had reduced prices when the price trend of strategic materials was upward, had given the government "100 per cent co-operation," but that Ickes in February had denied its request for additional power from the Bonneville dam in Oregon with which to manufacture more aluminum. Ickes had based his action on the ground that it was not the policy of the government to encourage monopolies. On this the committee, after its New Deal members had tried to suppress the report, said:

"Whatever may be the merits of any controversy between these so-called 'monopolies' and the Administration, it is the sense of this committee that a squabble at this time on the subject of monopoly is a tragic and sorry spectacle, indeed."

To cap the climax, a Federal Judge in New York in October ruled that the Government had not proved its charge against the Aluminum Company.

Also it developed that the New Deal's war on the power companies over a period of eight years was responsible for the crimped power facilities. The greatest power breakdown occurred in the famous Tennessee Valley project because of a drought. The private companies depending in part upon steam for their manufacture of power had all been run out of the area, and the TVA did not have adequate steam facilities. It came to light that the Securities and Exchange Commission was right then at the high point of executing the so-called "death sentence" of the Utilities Act of 1935 by which the private power industry had to be thoroughly overhauled. Naturally, the industry hadn't kept pace with even the normal increase in demands for power.

The SEC over the years had been the most important agency of the New Deal. From it came attacks on the utilities, on Wall Street, on insurance companies, and on what they considered the "old order" economic structure in general. It had served as a springboard for many a New Deal ambition. In connection with the Standard Gas and Electric Company receivership in 1939, forty New Dealers got handsome jobs in the receivership setup, including Leo Crowley, chairman of the Federal Deposit Insurance Corporation. From the commission, William O. Douglas went to the Supreme Court, Jerome Frank onto the bench of a lower court. Leon Henderson, a member of the commission, lost all interest in that job when the bigger defense game appeared. He just got up and walked away. In late July, in the midst of the power controversy, Mr. Roosevelt found the commission dangling in the bureaucratic maze with subordinates and secondary New Dealers in charge and administering the forced reorganization of the power industry. Thus, one of the most important defense industries in the country was in a state of confusion.

There was still another motive in the propaganda about aluminum. It was the New Dealers' determination to carry out the long-controverted St. Lawrence waterway and power project. It originated many years ago in New York state politics. Al Smith used to make it a vehicle of his state campaigns. Roosevelt embraced it while running for governor of New York. When Norris and the public power proponents succeeded in making the private power companies a national political issue with the 1929 collapse and subsequent exposures around Samuel Insull, Mid-West utilities tycoon, and other misdeeds of the utilities, the New Dealers put the St. Lawrence project in their program of fairly blanketing the country with vast government owned and operated power areas similar to the TVA. Inasmuch as the St. Lawrence project involved a treaty with Canada, ratification had to be obtained from the Senate, and that required a two-thirds vote. Mr. Roosevelt fell short of this vote when he submitted the treaty to the Senate in 1934. Making a new arrangement with his friend, the Canadian Premier, Mackenzie King, which he contended did not involve a treaty, he now pressed the project again as a defense necessity and requiring only a majority vote of Congress. Army engineers have estimated that it would take seven years to complete the project; the minimum estimates have been four years. An example of the efforts of Knudsen and Stettinius to get along with Washington's controversial elements was their endorsement of the project as essential to national defense. They did not really consider it to be. The building of this project would take steel and other metals, and money, necessary to defense.

As late as mid-August, an isolationist Washington newspaper, the Washington *Times-Herald,* and even some non-isolationist publications, printed stories that the British were selling American steel, which they had gotten from this country under the lend-lease bill, to South America. The British embassy took note of these reports and in a communication to the State Department said they were not true. It explained that American steel undoubtedly got into the processed products which Britain sold to South America to keep up its trade, which, the embassy said, American officials had agreed had to be done. The State Department, however, would not make the British embassy's explanation public, and after a delay of several weeks, the embassy made it public. Subsequently, at a press conference, Mr. Roosevelt indignantly attributed the reports about the British selling American lend-lease supplies to South America as the work of Hitler agents. Then he explained that the steel South America had been getting from Britain was that contracted for before the lend-lease bill was passed. There was no explanation from either him or the British embassy why this country, said to be facing a shortage of steel, was sending steel to Britain and Britain was selling steel to

South America. Others explained that it was necessary for Britain to keep up her dollar exchange. Maybe so.

On this sort of confused information—information produced by contentious men—priority orders were periodically issuing from the OPM under the signature of Stettinius, and industries in this country were being denied steel, aluminum and other metals essential to the conduct of their businesses. "Shortages" developed in such things as tooth paste; housewives couldn't get new faucets to stop the drip in their kitchen sinks. In countless instances, industries had been given priority ratings as being engaged in defense production. But in each delivery of metal they had to sign statements under oath that the particular order of metal they were getting was for defense production. In one actual instance of this kind—which could be multiplied thousands of times—the Ford Motor Company had only a few days' supply of aluminum on hand. Before the particular processing plant in Cleveland could ship the aluminum, there had to be the usual "release" from the OPM. At three o'clock of a Thursday afternoon, the Washington representative of the Cleveland plant was directed to go over to OPM and get the release. He was told that the plant had to sign and notarize the particular form required for such transactions. He communicated with his office and was told frantically that the form duly signed and notarized would be in Washington the following morning by airmail, special delivery. The following day, Friday, neither Knudsen, Stettinius, Biggers nor anyone else whom the Washington representative could find to be in authority was in the city, and no one else seemed to be able to find the letter. The release finally came Monday, and the Ford Motor Company got the aluminum barely in the nick of time. It was only one example of the confusion in Washington.

During the first week of July it occurred to Walter D. Fuller, president of the National Association of Manufacturers, to conduct a survey of twenty defense centers to ascertain whether shortage of aluminum was holding up defense production. The manufacturers' association had been greatly concerned about the intense propaganda being leveled at industry and industrialists. Many major industries were conducting an expensive magazine and radio advertising campaign to say they had readjusted their plants to serve America in time of need. Each defense center reported to Mr. Fuller that it was not experiencing a shortage of aluminum. Unfortunately for him, he made his findings public just as the government's nation-wide aluminum pots and pans collection campaign was getting under way. He was therefore denounced in a statement by the Office of Civilian Defense, the clear inference of the statement being that he and his fellow industrialists were Hitler lovers and saboteurs.

Then just as the pots and pans campaign ended, J. Louis Reynolds, vice-president of Reynolds Metal Products Company of Richmond, Virginia, whose firm was being financed by RFC to increase its aluminum production, calmly announced that he had sold 2,000,-

ooo pounds of the metal to the Russians. This 2,000,-
000 pounds, he explained, was part of an order of
3,000,000 pounds which had originally been sold to
France and then turned back. Since that time, Reynolds said, he had been unable to find a customer for it!

His brother, Richard H. Reynolds, president of the
company, had been the hero in the Truman committee's attack on the Aluminum Company several weeks
before. A New Dealer, Senator Lister J. Hill of Alabama,
produced him as a man who was willing to risk the
wrath of the giant Alcoa and, to save the country, go
into the rival production of aluminum. In the metal
products business the Reynoldses got their aluminum
from Alcoa. With government money they were prepared to challenge the giant.

At one point Hill asked if it were not true that he
had mortgaged all of his metal products companies in
this effort to help his country. He skipped the question.

Richard H. and J. Louis Reynolds are cousins of
Richard J. Reynolds, who contributed or "loaned"
some $300,000 to the New Deal 1940 campaign and
is now secretary of the Democratic National Committee.

In the army camps the soldiers were being served
syrup out of aluminum pitchers. The Navy Yard at
Norfolk, Virginia, advertised an auction of scrap aluminum! Then, as an added note, it developed that
nothing was being done with the collection of pots
and pans around the country. They were left in junk
heaps for weeks until local agitation developed. Then

in many instances the pots and pans were sold to processing firms to be made into new pots and pans!

Another interesting commentary on the New Dealers' contention of a power shortage, related to aluminum production, was the fact that the New Dealers themselves had been fighting for many months and were still holding up a program by which the government was to set up a series of power projects, similar to TVA, in Arkansas, the Columbia River Valley in Washington, the Upper Missouri Valley, and California. The struggle was between Ickes, Leland Olds, chairman of the Federal Power Commission, and the patriarchal New Dealer and father of public power enterprises, Senator George Norris of Nebraska. Ickes wanted control of the projects to be placed under him in the Department of the Interior, under an agency to be known as the "energy" administration; Olds wanted his Federal Power Commission to have control, and Norris wanted local officials to administer each project. Ickes was particularly incensed at Norris for opposing him, because in his award of millions of dollars of PWA funds to advance the public power cause, he gave some $60,000,000 to Nebraska for a project which flooded thousands of acres of farm lands and caused the farmers to rise in arms; so that eventually this controversial enterprise cost the government millions of additional dollars in placating outraged citizens.

That the President wanted to carry out these projects, however, on top of the defense program, brings up another commentary on the controversy about the shortage of defense material which these projects would have required. On top of the defense program, the New Deal had a spending program labeled as defense, the necessity of which was a serious question. Aside from the spending involved, it took essential defense materials. The amount of this questionable spending called for $5,783,232,000, as listed by the OPM, in the fiscal year beginning July 1, 1941. Probably half of it was not reflected in the over-all figure of some sixty billions which had been authorized for defense, because it was to be carried by financing of the RFC, whose operations were outside the budget. It included road building, housing, and sundry other projects which in numerous instances were New Deal reform enterprises. For example, $635,000,000 of this sum was allotted to so-called defense housing enterprises. Houses financed under this program costing from $3,000 to $4,000 required 4,000 pounds of steel, of which the OPM experts insisted 2,000 could be done away with; 142 pounds of copper, three-fourths of which could be done away with, and 77 pounds of zinc, whereas it was insisted seven pounds would be sufficient.

In 1939 Mr. Roosevelt effected a marked reorganization in his administrative setup, and in this he took the Public Works Administration (PWA) from Ickes, almost breaking his heart, and garnered up other building agencies, including the low-cost housing agency, United States Housing Administration under Nathan Straus, and various alley dwelling "authorities," the old WPA, and other loose agencies such as the Federal Fire Council, of which veteran reporters had never heard, under an organization to be known as the Federal Works Administration with W. J. Carmody as administrator. With the advent of spending for defense housing—that is, houses for the workers in the mushroom growth of defense plants, he set up an agency within his administration called the Defense Housing Division. His publicity men said he had become the biggest builder in the country, utilizing the regular agencies which he had already been administering, U. S. Housing, Alley Dwelling Authorities, WPA, and the Public Building Administration. It was not claimed, of course, that these agencies were actually erecting the buildings. They were just administering the projects, and on top of them the Defense Housing Division employed some 200 persons to administer these agencies.

In addition, Mrs. Roosevelt brought in Charles F. Palmer, an Atlanta real estate man, to act as co-ordinator of defense housing. The question of where his authority ended and Carmody's began was a continual cause of strife between them. In an outburst on one occasion Carmody charged Palmer with wasting time and money. He claimed that Palmer had forced him to take over a site in Boston to accommodate shipyard workers. Thirty days after the project had been completed, he said, not a single shipyard worker had moved into a house. Furthermore, he said, the site was more expensive than nearer sites.

"I used to think I knew what a 'co-ordinator' meant," Carmody shouted; "someone to get people to work together. I didn't know it was spelled 'd-i-c-t-a-t-o-r'."

Carmody as head of all the building agencies was supposed to be a co-ordinator himself. Palmer worked under the Office of Emergency Management administered by Wayne Coy, who reported to the President and Hopkins, and Palmer had 127 employees and an annual appropriation of $375,000. He declared on one occasion:

"The defense housing program in the United States at the present time is completing more houses per month than were completed by the British in 1938 at the peak of their public housing program."

That is exactly what the OPM, which had brought practically the entire industry of the country under its priorities, was complaining about. It was questioning not only the extent of the housing program but the amount of essential defense materials that was being used. This did not include the low-financed home building campaign which the Federal Housing Administration had been conducting for several years, nor the St. Lawrence seaway and water-power project, whose initial cost of $285,000,000 Mr. Roosevelt was urging Congress to authorize. To make sure of congressional authorization for this project, the President directed the congressional leaders to put it in the so-called omnibus Rivers and Harbors Bill. The annual Rivers and Harbors Bill has long been known as the "pork barrel," upon which Congressmen and Senators get together and vote for one another's pet projects to help to get themselves re-elected. In the omnibus bill along with the St. Lawrence project was one for carrying out the proposed ship canal across Florida, which called for an initial cost of $160,000,000 and had been several times turned down by Congress. Senator Claude Pepper was demanding it now because of his "all-out" aid to the administration and Britain.

On July 17, W. E. Reynolds, commissioner of public buildings, appeared before a closed meeting of a subcommittee of the House Appropriations Committee to explain an item of $6,000,000 which the Budget Bureau had approved for the building of temporary government offices on the outskirts of Washington. Representative Clifford A. Woodrum, of Virginia, third ranking man on the committee, asked him pleasantly if this would be enough, and then casually asked about a site which the War Department had acquired just across the river in Virginia for some relatively small temporary buildings for the War Department. A few days later, Brigadier General Brehon B. Somervell, of the Quartermaster's Department, reappeared with a set of plans for a permanent new War Department building to cost $35,000,000 and to cover thirty-five acres on the Virginia site.

It developed that Woodrum, together with Representative Howard D. Smith, representing the Virginia district just across the river, had gotten together with the Army officials to transfer the department out of the District of Columbia. In three weeks, over the protest of Mr. Roosevelt and the several agencies maintained to preserve Washington's symmetry and scenic effects, the bill was passed. Not a headquarters for the Army in this war alone, but for the next war, a building to house 40,000 persons. It was to be built in a year and thus was to further draw essential defense materials away from the job of defeating Hitler.

All or most government work got a priority preference, and all of this used, in varying amounts, essential defense materials. Yet out in the country industries and businesses were being closed down and men were being thrown out of work because the plants could not get a mite of metal or chemical or some other defense material for the particular gadgets they were manufacturing. The OPM estimated that the full impact of its priorities would close down between 5,000 and 6,000 industries.

Just as chemists develop nylon and plastics, the business of a man in political life is to develop "issues." In selling them to the public he is scarcely more concerned in their intrinsic worth than is the butcher in the meat or the bread he sells. Basically, the "issue" or merchant's ware is sold for just what the traffic will bear. And just as the merchant when he is selling meat is not thinking whether meat is just what the customer should eat, so the politician is not primarily concerned in whether his "issue" is helpful or harmful to the customer. A man who gets to thinking so unselfishly about his fellow man would likely never sell a piece of real estate, a suit of clothing, an "issue" or anything else. He would become so confused and overladen with the world on his shoulders that he would be pressed down in his tracks.

The industry of Washington being politics rather than the production of steel, of textiles or dairy products, the output is "issues." In recent years, more so than before, the highly inexact science of economics has become closely interwoven with the highly inexact science of politics. The Washington economists have become politicians, and those who frankly answered the description of "politician" in the past are wondering what is to become of them.

The Washington economist can prove anything and very often does. One will develop an "issue" out of the number of railroad carloadings that have taken place over a given period. Another economist will challenge him with the statement that so many inches have been taken off or put on the length of the cars in that period. The Department of Agriculture economists produce figures to show that two-thirds of the people of this country are undernourished. This is a decided improvement on the older statement that one-third of the people were undernourished. But the Department of Agriculture in this instance wants the farmers to put greater emphasis on dairy products, and less on wheat and cotton growing. The Secretary, Claude Wickard, a few years ago an obscure Indiana farmer, and up until a few months ago a relatively obscure official in the department, has made himself nationally known with the slogan that food will win the war and save the world.

Through the New Dealers' fight on the OPM, startling figures were produced to show that the defense program was bogging down. They were produced with the greatest of ease, like the acts of the man on the flying trapeze. On just what were they based? Who knew what the needs were?

Senators and members of the House sat around in their cloakrooms and discussed Mr. Roosevelt's plans and purposes with the same mingled objectivity and prejudice with which merchants discuss a fellow merchant who is getting more business than they. The isolationists openly accused Mr. Roosevelt of being a warmonger, of wanting to lead the country into war, but in the cloakrooms many of them complained, as did other non-New Dealers, that he was just "shrewd" enough not to do it. These men were convinced that if the country did get into a shooting war, the subsequent revulsion would, as they put it, "ride Roosevelt and the whole New Deal out of town on a rail." They were, therefore, worried that instead of "getting us into war" he would play his cards in the great poker game of international politics so as to come out as this country's savior and win a big place at the peace table, at that. Yet there were others, Democrats and New Dealers, to argue just as strongly that he was trying his best to lead the country into war. They pointed to such moves as the occupation of Iceland, the recurring agitation in administration circles for the seizure of Martinique and Dakar. Men who professed to be able to interpret Mr. Roosevelt's mind argued that he knew that sooner or later this country would have to send another expeditionary force to Europe; others professing to know his mind just as well, were convinced that he believed that if we gave England the bombers, the Germans could be bombed into submission.

Lord Beaverbrook, the British production minister, visiting in Washington in August, told Senators that the bombing premise was untenable, that it would take an army on the Continent to defeat Hitler, and that Britain couldn't furnish the army without this country's furnishing men.

In this confused situation, what were the economists basing their estimates of steel needs, aluminum needs, copper needs, on? Senator Tom Connally, chairman of the Senate Foreign Relations Committee, an all-out supporter of the President's foreign policy, told his colleagues in the cloakrooms, after the Lord Beaverbrook discussions, that he was in no mood to send troops and didn't think the President would be; that Britain had a way of getting other people to fight its fights.

It would require a tremendous lot more of steel and aluminum and copper and what-not for an army invading the Continent than to bomb Hitler into defeat. On what basis were estimates being made?

A highly significant fact was that all through the confusion, Mr. Roosevelt did not think the defense program was bogging down. He frequently said so. He knew what industry was producing; he alone knew the needs. Those 50,000 planes which a year before he had vividly described as blanketing our skies were nowhere in sight—scarcely one-tenth of them were. But did he really mean we were to have so many planes? Understatement has long since ceased to be a virtue in the affairs of public men. But, then, perhaps this statement was no more exaggerated than the example which the teachers in the graded schools used to give of the effects of alcohol on the human system: the pouring of alcohol on a piece of raw beef, causing it to turn black.

In the development of "issues," of "agitation," the man in political life can't afford to follow them through to their ultimate results. What he must do when they turn against him in the course of their weird spiral, is to develop other "issues" and "agitation" on top of them.

Then, what was to be the economic state of the country in September 1941 under the some sixty-billion-dollar defense appropriations as a result of the "issues" and counter "issues," the conflict of ambitious men, the resulting confusion?

It will probably never be known just what was the real state of employment in the country in 1940, but those who make a political living in Washington from what people out in the hinterlands produce, agreed as the opposing lawyers in a courtroom frequently do on a given proposition, on the figure of 10,000,000 unemployed. The New Dealers, the American Federation of

[99]

Labor leaders and the CIO leaders insisted this was the figure so as to justify additional government spending; the Republicans insisted it was to prove what mismanagers of government the New Dealers were.

Then, in the spring of '41, Secretary of Labor Perkins, by way of occasionally getting favorable instead of unfavorable mention in the press, made periodic statements about the number of persons that had been returned to employment. She got her estimates up, in the early summer, to a prediction that 5,000,000 of the unemployed would be absorbed by the first of the new year.

Then counter and highly discouraging figures began to issue from the government agencies in August. First, there was the accredited report that 175,000 persons in the silk industry were to be thrown out of employment as a result of our first "victory" over Japan, the declaration of an embargo; then the first week-end's operation of Ickes' 7 P.M. to 7 A.M. blackout on the sale of gasoline on the eastern seaboard was reported by Washington's accepted statisticians to have resulted in a 15 per cent increase in the consumption of gas but a 30 per cent reduction in employment. But far more important was the statement of OPM statisticians that more than 1,000,000 persons would be thrown out of work through the application of its priorities. Leon Henderson, the price administrator, blandly agreed when these figures began to be dangled around in the confusion of Washington that some

2,000,000 persons necessarily would be thrown out of work as part of the sacrifice the American people had to make to crush Hitler. Yet the statistics also showed America's productive output at the highest in its history! With monthly government expenditures higher than at the very height of the First World War, with industrial output higher, employment was being *created!*

It was, of course, just as impossible to get accurate figures on this subject as on the number of unemployed in 1940. But the Works Projects Administration, directly under Howard O. Hunter, had figures at the same time showing a far more serious picture. Of course it, too, had a motive. Supposed to give relief to the unemployed, its appropriation for the fiscal year beginning July 1 was cut from $1,350,000,000 to $850,000,000 annually. It was conducting an energetic campaign among the country's editors to convince them that the defense spending was making no appreciable dent in unemployment. But as of August, it wouldn't release its figures on unemployment for general consumption for fear of running up against the wrath of Miss Perkins, who had been painting a roseate picture of employment. It confined itself to a quiet campaign among the editors.

The WPA economists had worked out a study, just as convincing as any other such studies floating around bureaucratic Washington, to show that there were 8,000,000 unemployed at the beginning of 1941, and that only 1,500,000, if not less, would be absorbed by

January 1, 1942, leaving 6,500,000 still unemployed. These economists prepared a formula to show that defense employment was creating unemployment.

In the emergency year of 1941, as for many years past, the Washington bureaucrats looked upon the more than 130,000,000 citizens of the country as statistics, and frequently, to carry their point, they split them into parts. Where the exact truth lay no one knew.

But the evidence was overwhelming, from the thousands of letters coming to Congressmen, that out in the country people were getting hurt—not from the necessity of beating Hitler but from the agitation and confusion of Washington. Small businesses were protesting loudly—and in vain. During the more than four months when Henderson was fighting with the OPM over the application of priorities, very few permits were issued to non-defense industries to get any left-over essential defense materials that existed. Or did any exist?

On the basis of the agitation about shortages, priorities gobbled up everything in sight.

CHAPTER VI

Labor Leaders and Communists

In World War No. 1, it was not uncommon for cracker-barrel groups around the country to observe solemnly that it seemed pretty certain that Woodrow Wilson was going to turn over the country to Samuel Gompers. They were wrong. The grim-visaged Presbyterian President of those days, on occasion, really called in the veteran head of the American Federation of Labor to read the riot act to him.

In 1941 there were people just as certain that Mr. Roosevelt was determined to turn the country over to organized labor. But a great difference, and one that constituted no small part of the confusion which hung over the country's defense effort, was that even if he were so minded there was no Gompers or any other single labor head to whom the deed could be delivered. Bitterness and fighting among the labor leaders was as intense as that between the New Dealers and the Dollar-a-Year men.

First, there was the bitterness between the Federation and the CIO.

Second, there was the bitterness within the Federation's own high ranks.

Third, there was the bitterness within the CIO's own high ranks.

On top of this was John L. Lewis' bitter hostility to Mr. Roosevelt and his open opposition to the war effort, and in return, the attitude of Mr. Roosevelt and the New Dealers toward Lewis, based on their conviction that he was just about the worst ingrate ever to breathe democracy's pure air.

Over all was the suspicion with which the leaders of both the AFL and CIO regarded Sidney Hillman, who sat alongside of Knudsen at the top of OPM. And adding to this confusion was the feeling of Frances Perkins, Secretary of Labor, that after she had built up Hillman, he had wrested the labor custodianship entirely from her.

When the New Dealers set up the NRA in 1933, Lewis' coal miners' union had been on the rocks for several years. Moving quickly under the impetus of the New Deal, he restored it, and although a Republican in the past, he now joined in the socio-political crusade which was getting under way. Sharpening up his ability to use Shakespearean phrases, he became chummy with the ruling Intellectuals and ran around with them at night. Notwithstanding his rock-bottom political conservativeness, he would nod agreement when the Intellectuals talked in such advanced terms that he didn't know what they were talking about. On the other hand, the Intellectuals couldn't warm up to unadventurous, plodding William Green, president of the American

Federation of Labor. The Federation leaders, generally, recalled the earlier labor movements, such as the Knights of Labor, which came to no good end when they strayed from the path of labor's own selfish interests and tied up with crusades. From the time of Gompers on, the Federation's policy was to eye political movements dispassionately and solely in the interest of labor, to play the Democrats against the Republicans and vice versa. For example, the Federation always supported the high protective tariff policy of the Republicans. One exception to the general rule was when the Federation endorsed the presidential candidacy of the late Senator Robert M. LaFollette in 1924.

As the New Dealers uttered coined slogans about the "Forgotten Man" and the "Redistribution of Wealth," Green and his aides remained unmoved. When they had a particular problem they took it up just as they had done with governments in the past. The New Dealers decided they were too lacking in imagination to fit into the New Order. In their way they were as bad as the Reactionary Employers, the New Dealers concluded, and soon they were advertising this.

They took Lewis, and with a magician-like manipulation of their hands and the intonation of magic words, declared him henceforth to be a "Liberal" regardless of his past. They boosted his CIO, with Hillman as one of the real labor "intellectuals" working in the background, and set out with it to destroy the leadership of Green and the other Federation leaders. The

[105]

New Deal's vast propaganda machinery and WPA funds built up the CIO and Lewis. Is it any wonder that they felt bitter toward him when he first split with the President and subsequently supported Wendell Willkie?

In the spring of 1941, next to the Communists he was their greatest problem in the labor situation.

There was a time—in the steel strikes of 1937—when Lewis and Hillman and even the New Dealers were as one in using a slogan:

"If the employers hire Communists, we will accept them in the CIO."

The employers, under the circumstances, had no choice in the matter of those they employed.

But when Lewis split with the New Dealers they built up Hillman against him. Miss Perkins introduced Hillman to the New Deal in the NRA days. To advance him further against Lewis, he was brought into the high labor key place in the first defense setup, in May of 1940. Thus fortified, he was able to go to the New York State Convention of the American Labor Party a few months later and hold the "conservative" wing of this Leftist organization in line for Mr. Roosevelt, and to force Lewis into leadership of the Communist bloc. From that time Hillman, with the New Dealers' support, came to be the dominant influence, on the "conservative" side, of the CIO, which was certainly to the left of center itself; and Lewis, the former Republican whom the New Dealers turned into a "Liberal" in the manner in which Punjab in the Little Orphan Annie comic strip made people evaporate, found himself the leader of radicals and avowed Communists.

Hillman was one of the shrewdest men—perhaps the shrewdest of all—engaged in the American labor movement. Other men seek power through the acquisition of dollars, which gives them a hold over men; Hillman sought power through the direct control of men.

He was born and spent his earlier years in Russia, coming to this country through those floodgates of Eastern European immigration around the turn of the century when industrialists were seeking labor. His wife was a protégée of the anarchist, Emma Goldman. On a trip to Soviet Russia, the Soviet organ *Pravda* referred to him as "Comrade." Upon his return he wrote glowingly of seeing the hammer and sickle emblems in the plants of Mussolini's earlier Italy.

But he was no Communist. Instead, he had risen to labor power by kicking Communist rivals out—because they were rivals, however, rather than because they were Communists. His whole background was that of brutal labor politics, out of which he rose to be absolute czar of the Amalgamated Clothing Workers, centered in New York and made up 100 per cent of Eastern European immigrant origin. They constituted virtually a self-sufficient island in this country's heterogeneous make-up, over which Hillman was the supreme ruler. He voted them as he pleased, he levied assessments on them to support a candidate for public office of his choosing, as he did for Mr. Roosevelt in the 1936 and 1940 presidential campaigns. In turn, he saw that they got adequate clothing, food, medical care and recreation.

In the way in which labels had been tossed around in recent years, he was described as a Conservative, as, indeed, he was. He would have liked a setup whereby one employer employed all of the men in the country and he furnished the men. Then he and the employer could work harmoniously together; there would never need be any trouble between them at all. The strife between Capital and Labor would be eliminated. He called this "stabilization."

He had gotten no further along on this road than his Amalgamated Clothing Workers until, under Mr. Roosevelt's wing, he advanced to national eminence. As he operated from his key position in the defense setup, Phil Murray, the CIO leader, John L. Lewis and the American Federation of Labor leaders eyed him suspiciously. This situation was partly responsible for the labor trouble in the defense industries.

In the late spring Communist and Leftist inspired strikes were rampant in defense industries. Government officials estimated at the time that 20 per cent of the strikes were of Communist origin, while of the remainder, 60 per cent were prolonged by Communist agitation. Regardless of the accuracy of these figures, the State Department was in the anomalous position of trying to convince Stalin, through his Washington ambassador, Constantin Oumansky, that Hitler was his enemy and that he should co-operate in our defense production program. This, in spite of the provision in the agreement by which our government recognized the Soviets in 1933, that the latter, as a condition to the agreement, would not propagandize in this country.

The American people, as reflected by their Congress, were demanding action to stop these strikes. At their very height Miss Perkins was out in the West making speeches. Along with the general practice of Washington officialdom, she charged for her speeches and, at $500 a speech, appreciably added to her income as a cabinet member.

She considered that Hillman took advantage of her absence when at his instance the President set up a special Mediation Board. It was composed, as usual with such boards, of representatives of the "employer," of "labor," and of the "public." Hillman was to exercise a considerable influence over the board through Isador Lubin, a Department of Labor statistician elevated to the rank of "brain truster." There were such conservatives on the board as Eugene Meyer, multimillionaire publisher of the *Washington Post*. These men, serving on a board, have a horror of being accused of anything like holding up national defense. Labor leaders are not so sensitive. Furthermore, when they are serving on a mediation board they have constituencies continually on their necks. The representatives of industry, unless their particular industry is involved, have no one to answer to. Under such circumstances with the setting up of the Mediation Board, it was downright negligence on the part of the labor leaders not to demand a fifteen or twenty-five per cent increase for their men and threaten to strike, in the expectation of getting half of their demands.

Out of forty-five cases that had come before the board in late July it had ordered increases in thirty-two, had denied increases in none. In one instance it ordered the employer to accept the outright closed shop, under which he cannot employ a man unless he is a member in good standing with a union, and must discharge him if he does not remain in good standing.

One particular action of this board, manipulated by Hillman and Lubin, made history. Through it, Hillman was to hit two birds with one stone.

At the time, Lewis was admittedly encouraging the strikes in the defense industries. When the Mediation Board was set up, he counseled his followers to have nothing to do with it. They wouldn't get a square deal from Hillman's creation, he advised.

Also, at the time, a vote ordered by the National Labor Relations Board among the employees of the Ford plant was impending. The Ford officials were plainly confident of the outcome. Over the preceding years the CIO had succeeded in organizing other automobile and steel plants, but Ford remained unshaken in his determination not to recognize the union.

So Hillman and R. J. Thomas, head of the CIO automobile workers' union, got together, and it was arranged that the latter should demand a 10 per cent increase in wages and a closed shop of General Motors. The case came before the Mediation Board, which granted the 10 per cent increase but denied the closed shop request. It was utterly futile, after that decision, for Lewis to counsel his followers that they could get nothing from the board, and what was more important, it destroyed Ford's argument to his employees that he gave better pay than the CIO could get them. A few weeks later the CIO overwhelmingly won the Ford election. The automobile magnate who had so stubbornly fought unionism, capitulated.

Lewis, however, remained hostile to the board, and his West Coast followers, in the aviation and lumber industries, continued to defy it until Mr. Roosevelt sent troops into the North American aviation plant in California, and then a few weeks later Hitler turned on Stalin and the word went down the Communist party line to support the President.

In this play, Miss Perkins was practically shorn of any power over labor. In the executive order creating the Mediation Board it was provided that the board could not take jurisdiction in a labor dispute unless she certified it to that agency. She showed no inclination to do this. Whereupon, Senator Harry M. Byrd of Virginia arose on the floor of the Senate and demanded to know why she did not. It was apparent from the temper of his colleagues that they were prepared publicly to censure America's first woman cabinet member. She quickly certified four cases and con-

tinued to certify all except the more or less routine
ones. In the spring of 1940, Mr. Roosevelt, to check
the growing storm in Congress over her permitting
the indiscriminate flow of refugees into the country,
removed the Bureau of Immigration from her jurisdiction and placed it with the Department of Justice.
Thus, although she now presided over a tremendous
marble structure, she was Secretary in name only and
devoted her work mostly to dealing with philosophical labor matters, such as humanitarian legislation, at
which she excelled and was quite advanced.

The mail of Congressmen still reported that the
people out in the country felt that Miss Perkins and
Ickes were Mr. Roosevelt's two greatest liabilities. But
Mrs. Roosevelt stuck to the former and Mr. Roosevelt
stuck to the latter, even through the confusion they
caused.

Lewis continued his war on Hillman after the West
Coast strikes were settled, but his harassing tactics
were admittedly reduced when his Communist followers went in for all-out aid to the "democracies."

Lewis, when he announced his support of Wendell
Willkie in an impassioned radio speech just a few
weeks before the close of the 1940 campaign, promised that if Willkie did not win he would resign his
presidency of the CIO. After the campaign Hillman
pursued him and he was forced to fulfill this promise.
Philip Murray, head of the steel workers, was named
in his place. In the ensuing months Lewis' friends con-

tended that Murray was Lewis' man. Hillman's followers, on the other hand, insisted he was Hillman's man. The fact seemed to be that although Murray did keep Lewis' appointees in the places they had held in the CIO, he nevertheless tried to walk a straight line between Hillman and Lewis. Then in the summer of 1941 he fell ill.

This increased the tension between the two rival forces as the time for the CIO's annual convention in the fall approached. Every indication pointed toward Lewis' seeking to regain the dominant position in the CIO, and his grounds were to be that Mr. Roosevelt and Hillman were selling out labor and leading the country into war. In midsummer it was his custom to pace up and down the floor of his ornate offices just a few blocks from the White House and make these charges to anyone who wanted to come and listen. It seemed but a matter of time before he made them publicly.

As it was, his agitation had the effect of keeping Hillman in a hot seat, causing him to be more cantankerous in his dealings with Stettinius and Knudsen as well as other defense officials. In other words, instead of playing the part of a statesman in a national emergency, he had frequently to turn to meet Lewis' agitation among his constituents.

For example, Lewis, to have an "issue" against Hillman, kept agitating that Labor was not really being given a voice in the defense program, that it just looked as though it was. The country at large would undoubtedly have been surprised to know that Labor was being given the run-around. Lewis demanded that employer-employee committees be set up for each industry along the lines of the NRA codes. To meet this agitation, Hillman with Knudsen set up joint employer-employee advisory committees for the countless commodities with which OPM was dealing. The inescapable result was to add more and more bickering personalities in every decision that had to be made.

Even then, Lewis insisted that this plan was but a subterfuge and advised his followers to have nothing to do with it. Hillman had difficulty getting a representative group from the CIO.

Miss Perkins, because of her antipathy to Hillman, set up a Labor National Advisory Committee in opposition to the system Hillman was trying to effect. Green co-operated with her against the advice of other Federation leaders, notably William K. Hutcheson. Green opposed Hillman himself.

But the Building Trades Council, the most influential branch of the Federation, with Hutcheson as a dominant figure, had sized up Hillman cautiously after his appointment and then struck a bargain with him by which Hillman agreed upon closed shops for the building trades in the erection of all army camps and other defense building. So the council repudiated Green's action.

As to how the bargain worked out, a look-in at Camp Meade, Maryland, and Camp Blanding, Florida, is revealing. At the former, of the 8,113 workers listed as carpenters, 55 per cent were what might be called rough carpenters and 35 per cent were not carpenters at all.

Both camps were built on a closed-shop basis for both skilled and common labor. Non-union carpenters had to pay $57.50 initiation fees. They could get a work permit from the union by agreeing that half of the fee could be taken out of their first week's pay. Common laborers had to pay a $25 initiation fee.

Miss Perkins is empowered by law to fix the wage scales for these building projects. Notwithstanding that Camp Meade is just the same distance from Washington in Maryland as Fort Belvoir is in Virginia, she applied different scales. Carpenters at Camp Meade received $1.25 an hour, at Fort Belvoir $1.62½ an hour. Electricians received $1.50 an hour at Camp Meade, and $1.80 an hour at Fort Belvoir.

The result was that in an effort to hold the better workers, the contractor at Camp Meade had to throw in Saturday and Sunday overtime at time and a half and double pay to make up for the difference in scales.

At the peak of construction at Camp Blanding, 21,-300 men were employed, of whom 5,000 were classified as carpenters. Approximately 50 per cent of the latter were really carpenters while the remaining 50 per cent had had very little, if any, experience. If they did not belong to the union they, too, had to pay the "initiation" fees.

One day, C. E. Bush, assistant business agent of the asbestos workers' union, Jacksonville, Florida, local

No. 13, came into the camp and pulled thirteen asbestos workers off their jobs because they did not belong to the union. Bush and four other workers of Jacksonville had organized the local a year before by paying $25 to the national organization for a charter. The local still had only eight members, including Bush and his four associates. They charged $50 for initiation fees. Instances of this kind went on in the camps all over the country. Millions of dollars were added to the union coffers; in some instances, the money went into the pockets of racketeer leaders. At Camp Edwards, Massachusetts, Miss Perkins boosted the wage scale once and then the subcontractors boosted it again, until it was 61.5 per cent higher than the prevailing wages at New Bedford, near by. The contractors built the camp on the cost-fee basis, by which all costs are charged to the government.

Lewis and William L. Hutcheson, head of the carpenters' union, met frequently to further their war on Green.

Hutcheson and Lewis were running mates back in the Republican days. Hutcheson had remained a Republican and, if possible, felt even more bitter toward Mr. Roosevelt than Lewis. Once, while Lewis was a New Dealer, they had an argument at the annual convention of the Federation, and Lewis struck Hutcheson in the jaw. But now they were back together, and should they be able to combine their forces and become the dominant labor figures they would add to

Mr. Roosevelt's problems, particularly those relating to his foreign policy. But on the latter point organized labor, as reflected in its publications, seemed to be viewing Mr. Roosevelt through critical eyes. The weekly organ of the Big Four brotherhoods, *Labor,* published in Washington, and probably the most influential labor periodical, continued its undiminished support of Senator Wheeler and other isolationists. It gave prominence to Lindbergh's utterances, and while it still referred endearingly to "F.D." on domestic matters, it spoke scornfully of "warmongers." Secretaries Knox and Stimson were frequently singled out for attack.

It was a tremendous boon for Britain when Hitler turned against Stalin, but perhaps it would have been better for this country's internal problems had he held off a few more weeks.

After eight years of coddling Communists, the government in the spring seemed to be definitely moving against them. The love which had obtained between the New Dealers and the disciples of Moscow turned into hate when the latter refused to go along with the President's all-out aid policy in 1939.

But no move was made toward getting them out of the government until early spring of 1941. It was not to be expected that there would be any such move during the campaign, because the New Dealers had insisted all along that there were no Communists among them. They had heaped ridicule on the famous Dies Committee. Ickes and Mrs. Roosevelt had been the leaders in this. Several persons who had been branded by name as Communists were held by the New Dealers to be nothing more than advanced Liberals. It professedly amused them no end that Liberals should be thought to be Communists. The term "fellow traveler," adopted by the Dies Committee for those about whom it had pretty justifiable suspicions which nevertheless could not be pinned down, was a particular subject of mockery for the New Dealers.

"What is a fellow traveler?" they would teasingly ask. "You mean a fellow who has been seen with a Communist or who has merely read a Communist book?"

But now that they had come to be "red baiters" they bandied around the term "fellow traveler" as much as the Dies Committee ever did.

A typical case was that of Edwin S. Smith, member of the National Labor Relations Board. A congressional investigation in the spring of 1940, conducted by the Smith Committee under the Congressman of that name from Virginia, revealed that the NLRB was honeycombed with Communists and their sympathizers. Under such an administration, this board was generally considered by Congress to have been directly responsible for the reign of lawlessness which began with the sit-down strikes of 1937 and which probably brought on the so-called recession of that year. Set up primarily to insure a man his right to join a union of his own choosing, the NLRB, as revealed by the Smith Committee, had been deliberately stirring up strife in industry.

One of the first things the administration did when it moved against the Communists in the spring was to purge the NLRB. Edwin S. Smith's term did not expire until late August, but it was made very plain at this time that he was not to be reappointed.

"Is he really a Communist?" conservatives would now ask their New Deal friends.

"Well, if he isn't one, he might as well be," they would reply indignantly. "At least, he is a fellow traveler."

Ever since the NLRB was created, the conservatives had been insisting this was exactly the case.

In this housecleaning, Nathan Straus, head of the U. S. Housing Administration, was seemingly hurt to find that in his agency was Ben Ades, who ran for Governor of Maryland on the Communist ticket in 1938. Miss Perkins similarly came across the case of Helen Miller. Both were dismissed as Communists. The WPA dismissed David Lasser, and there were many Washington observers who thought this young man was a victim of the New Dealers' anti-Communist zeal. Earlier in the New Deal, Lasser, only a few years out of Harvard, joined with Herbert Benjamin, an avowed and active Communist, in the racket of organizing the WPA workers at 25 cents a head per month. Benjamin was the "executive secretary," and unquestionably the dominating influence. Lasser always denied that he himself was a Communist. Hopkins recognized the organization as a bona-fide representation of the WPA workers. In 1939 Lasser and Benjamin had a quarrel and Lasser went to work for the government. Now he was dismissed as a fellow traveler in the great New Deal red hunt in the spring of 1941.

As a part of the wave, Mrs. Roosevelt freely told friends that she had been wrong in coddling the Communist-dominated American Youth Congress. She had thought they were simply frustrated youngsters and that she could straighten them out, she explained.

This enthusiastic soap-scrubbing of the New Deal was going on when Hitler turned on Stalin in June. Hillman and Murray had been persuaded, the latter more reluctantly, to run the Communists out of official positions in the CIO.

The policy toward Communists changed almost overnight. Communist Ambassador Oumansky showed up at the State Department all smiles. Only a few weeks previously, Secretary of State Cordell Hull had called him in and talked in strong language about Communist activities in defense industries. The ambassador and his predecessor, M. Troyanovsky, had been Washington's most extravagant diplomatic hosts up until the New Dealers and the Communists split. The embassy parties, under glittering chandeliers and with unlimited supplies of caviar and champagne, were the capital's most brilliant gatherings. Then came the long siege in the dog house for Oumansky—Troyanovsky had gone back to Moscow. The curtains were drawn. There were no parties.

A few days after Oumansky's smiling and happy visit to the State Department, the embassy lights once again shone brilliantly, and stylishly attired guests drew up in a seemingly endless procession of chauffeured cars. Another scene reminiscent of the Czar's court at St. Petersburg had come.

If all of this was not enough to add to the confusion of Washington, one could rest assured that the continued presence of Communists in the government would. Notwithstanding that they were under orders to support the policy of all-out aid to the "democracies," the rank and file of American Communists are constitutionally opposed to co-operating in an office or plant in which they are working. By nature they are "office politicians" and grievance manufacturers. They were, as in the past, to find continual cause for agitation—shorter hours, more pay, better typewriter ribbons. Many of the government offices were hotbeds of Leftist labor agitation, and workers' committees were frequently waiting on department heads and ferreting out grievances.

In August, Leon Henderson, appearing before the House Banking and Currency Committee in connection with a bill to give statutory standing to his price-fixing status, was asked about one Tom Tippett working in his office and said by the Dies committee to be a fellow traveler.

Henderson retorted that Dies was not a responsible member of Congress and that he would not be guided by any findings of his committee. This was an example of the conflict between department heads and the government's law-making branch at a time when national unity was being sought.

CHAPTER VII

The Eccles-Morgenthau Feud

WITH Washington literally wallowing in defense billions, its most important agencies necessarily were those dealing with the nation's finance. Resting upon a delicate perch as the governmental financial structure did, it would seem to be fundamental that there be the closest co-operation between Secretary of the Treasury Henry Morgenthau and Governor Marriner S. Eccles of the Federal Reserve Board. Yet it was with the utmost difficulty that they treated each other civilly.

Their running fight had continued ever since they assumed their respective positions, and there were not the slightest signs of its abating in the National Emergency. Instead, this only quickened their desire for power. Close examination of the record does not reveal one single agreement between them on a major issue over a period of some eight years. Instead of the close synchronization called for in the very nature of the Treasury and the Reserve system, such a feeling existed between the two men that each saw ulterior motives in almost any proposal the other advanced.

On one occasion, the news tickers in the government departments at the Capitol and the National Press Club carried the brief announcement apropos of Morgenthau's going off to inspect his Coast Guard fleet:

"Henry Morgenthau is at sea."

Official Washington liked to crack jokes at Morgenthau's expense, and in this instance it got a really good laugh.

"What's news about Henry being at sea?" Senators, government officials and newspapermen nudged one another and asked, and everybody within hearing laughed. But the laugh quickly froze on Eccles' face as his hatred of the Treasury Secretary came to the surface.

Eccles served under Morgenthau for a few months when the latter took over the Treasury in November 1933, and he did not form a good impression of his chief. His impression didn't improve with time, and as he moved around at the cocktail and dinner parties of the official and semi-official set, he didn't hesitate to say that it didn't. The feeling was mutual, and since Morgenthau lost a lot of his timidity with his increasing power, he was given periodically to paying his disrespects publicly to Eccles. A movement was started in Congress in the early summer to investigate the feud between the two men because of its relation to the lives of some 130,000,000 citizens in times of stress, but it was squelched in its earliest stages.

Eccles started the fight, but what Morgenthau did to him afterwards was reflected in his frequent lament:

"A monetary system divided against itself cannot stand," he said.

Mr. Roosevelt's appointment of his fellow squire of Hyde Park to be the Treasury Secretary bowled over many of the country's monetary-minded citizens. Morgenthau had been serving as head of the Farm Credit Bureau, and his ambition was to be Secretary of Agriculture, inasmuch as he had had some farm experience in New York, particularly on his own place.

But then when the President named Eccles as the country's co-money authority the financial community felt that the world had come to an end. Eccles inherited a Utah banking chain, but bankers insisted that if his banks were operated the way he talked at the time, he would not have any banks very long. He was one of the first financial wizards on the scene when Mr. Roosevelt took office, and in those history-making days the babel of tongues seeking recognition was perhaps even louder than it was in the defense bureaucracy. One had to yell real loud and say something unusually shocking to attract attention, and Eccles did this. He called a huge national debt a blessing; he was one of the earliest apostles of spending and more spending on the part of the government; he advocated inflationary powers in the hands of the President. All of this literally made Morgenthau wince. He was inherently conservative, notwithstanding that his father never thought highly of his ability to handle money.

Henry Ford was down to see Mr. Roosevelt on one occasion, and at the White House he met Eccles. The latter, fox-like, of slight build, but a daring talker and doer, expounded his unorthodox economic theories at such length that the automobile magnate was fascinated.

En route to New York later in the afternoon, Ford kept asking a traveling companion:

"What did you say that little fellow's name was?"

Then he would shake his head in amused wonderment.

Eccles said later that all he did was to recall to Ford, Macaulay's *History of England*, which, according to Eccles, "recalled the fallacious reasoning which existed in England more than a century ago regarding the national debt."

Whatever was said caused Ford long to remember Eccles, even if he did frequently have to ask his name.

Morgenthau once likened Eccles' brand of economics to playing the races—this after he got up to the point of talking back to his critics.

Their feud got down to real, careful planning on both sides when Eccles worked with Senator Carter Glass, in the passage of the Banking Act of 1935, to have Morgenthau removed as ex-officio member of the Federal Reserve Board. Inasmuch as the Treasury Secretary had served in this capacity ever since the board was created under Woodrow Wilson, this was right humiliating. In those days it looked as though anybody could pick on Morgenthau, and undoubtedly Eccles felt cocky; but the subsequent record indicates that he was on the losing end of the fight.

The business of the Treasury is to raise money, through borrowing or taxation, and to pay the government's bills. The Federal Reserve Board, on the other hand, is in charge of the banking and credit system. Through various controls it is charged with keeping just the right flow of money and credit in the country. Morgenthau moved in on Eccles to such an extent that he could nullify many of the board's activities; and conversely, Eccles could at least embarrass him.

When the war broke out in September 1939, Eccles went into the open market and bought government bonds to the extent of $400,000,000 for the purpose of holding up their price. This is outright rigging of the market but legal when done by the government.

Morgenthau was interested in the price of bonds from day to day, because in always having to borrow, he could figure what his next loan would cost him. Eccles didn't tell him what he was doing, and for several days Morgenthau was jubilantly watching the stock ticker under the impression that the bonds were holding up without artificial support. When he learned the facts, he hot-footed it to Mr. Roosevelt and registered a bitter complaint. Apparently nothing was done, however.

With the advent of the defense spending, Eccles concluded that interest rates, generally, should go up as one of the deterrents against inflation. Ordinarily his Reserve Board could bring this about by calling upon the banks to increase their excess reserve requirements, thus restricting their free money. But Morgenthau had

a lever over him with the two-billion-dollar stabilization fund, and he threatened to use this fund to buy
government bonds from the banks, thus giving them
more cash, if Eccles tried to send interest rates up.
Naturally, Morgenthau didn't want to have to pay
more for his government borrowings, and there was
this serious question: When and if interest rates did
go up, how could the interest payments on the huge
and steadily mounting government debt be carried?
Yet the abnormally low rates have had a tremendous
effect on the country's economy. They have affected
everyone with money to invest, property holders, and
particularly insurance policy holders.

A man who had bought a house under the higher
interest rates now found that his house had been depre-
ciated in value by the new houses built with cheaper
money. Similarly, he did not get as much money on
his investments. In the case of insurance policy holders
of mutual companies, their dividends were reduced, in
some instances practically eliminated, because of the
reduced return the companies got on their investments.

The stabilization fund was one of the most powerful instruments a government official ever had. It con-
sisted of the profit accruing to the government when
the President devalued the dollar to 59 cents. As to
what was done with it, that was pretty much Morgenthau's own secret. Before the war he manipulated it to
stabilize the currencies of France and Great Britain,
and he claimed that this operation ended with a profit

to the government of some $20,000. The only use to which it had been put since the war, so far as publicly known, was that $100,000,000 was set aside to stabilize the currencies of China and the Argentine.

Eccles sought to get this Damocles sword from over his head at the 1941 session of Congress. Early in the year he recommended that Morgenthau be required at least to consult with the Reserve Board before using the stabilization fund against its operations. He also asked for a wider range in which he could move the banks' reserve requirements up and down so as to be in a better position to combat Morgenthau and get the interest rates up. Furthermore, he asked that Congress revoke the emergency monetary powers which were in the hands of the President but which came under Morgenthau's jurisdiction. Among the powers he wanted to revoke was that one authorizing a further devaluation of the dollar, which, for one thing, would add to Morgenthau's stabilization fund. Eccles showed his recommendations to the President, who made no objection to their being sent to Congress. Morgenthau didn't know about them.

Eight days after Eccles had submitted these recommendations, Morgenthau publicly declared the former's action had caused a "substantial and unwarranted decline" in the price of government bonds.

"It looks as if we will have to pay more for the next $500,000,000 of defense bonds," he complained bitterly.

A mischievous reporter asked him if he thought the Eccles recommendations might be "an attempt to take control of the money market from the government and give it back to New York bankers."

"It raises an interesting thought," Morgenthau replied.

It also raised an interesting thought that one New Dealer should entertain such an idea about a fellow New Dealer when they were both supposed to be working so unselfishly to defeat Hitler.

Morgenthau went quickly to work and within a few weeks, with Mr. Roosevelt's support, had succeeded in killing the Eccles recommendations in Congress.

The record was that in the six days following Eccles' proposals, the price of government bonds did drop, one representative issue falling off as much as three points. It didn't affect the average bondholder unless he happened to be selling his bonds those particular days, but for the big operators millions of dollars turn over on these operations.

Eccles plaintively asserted that the "Federal Reserve System finds itself in the position of being unable effectively to discharge all of its responsibilities," but with the President on the side of Morgenthau he couldn't get any relief from Congress.

The Morgenthaus and the Roosevelts are close personal friends. Although Morgenthau had become bolder, he was still very sensitive. Usually he lunched with the President every Monday, at which time he poured out his woes. If he wasn't called for lunch on this particular day, he fretted until he could find out a reason.

The country, having become fairly shock-proof, probably paid little or no attention to the spectacle of three different government agencies fighting before Congress in 1941 over the shape the three-billion-dollar tax bill should take. Ordinarily, the Treasury is responsible for formulating the administration's tax program, and nothing in opposition is heard from the executive branch of the government. As the bill comes from the Treasury it is the official version of the executive branch.

But in the conflict and turmoil of 1941 Washington, both Eccles and Henderson were appearing in opposition to some of the basic features of Morgenthau's bill. Their justification lay in their respective concern with the question of inflation.

Early in August, just as the House Ways and Means Committee was finishing the draft of a tax bill, Mr. Roosevelt wrote to the venerable chairman, Robert L. Doughton of North Carolina, suggesting some changes. This was too much for one of Mr. Roosevelt's stanchest supporters. The North Carolinian, refusing to change the bill, wrote back and in the course of his letter said:

"I am surprised to learn that your views are antagonistic to those expressed so emphatically by the Treasury as the representative of the administration. The committee at times found it impossible during the course of its hearings to reconcile the testimony of different officials representing the administration."

The feeling between Eccles and Morgenthau was rather strikingly reflected when Eccles once made a speech to a group of St. Louis bankers in which he proposed a tax plan. He said it was only a suggestion on his part. The following day a Treasury spokesman snapped:

"I don't think he spoke for the administration. I doubt seriously if he spoke for Congress. I am certain he didn't speak for the Treasury."

Eccles had made it plain he was not speaking for anyone of these three. The probability is he was just making a speech.

In the running fight between him and Morgenthau they both occasionally looked over their shoulders to see the threatening shadow of Jesse Jones and his tremendous money-lending powers, but they couldn't get him into controversy. He simply wouldn't controverse.

Several times Morgenthau told him that he thought the RFC ought to be in the Treasury when it got around to the liquidating stage, which, of course, was not in sight. Jones, with his angelic face, in each instance agreed that this should be, and then slyly added:

"Of course, I'll be Secretary of the Treasury then."

This always momentarily unnerved Morgenthau.

Jones is one of the most remarkable men ever to serve in Washington. He gradually spread out his control until he had some twenty government agencies under him. In 1940 the New Dealers sought to ease him away from the tremendously powerful Federal Loan Administration, which in turn administered the RFC, the Federal Housing Administration, the Export-Import Bank, the Surplus Commodities Corporation and the like, by dangling a cabinet office, the Secretary of Commerce, before him. He simply took over the Commerce Secretaryship in addition to his other agencies.

Congress, by and large, encouraged him to do this, because in Washington Jones stood out in all the confusion as a shining beacon of calmness and administrative ability, and the agencies over which he presided were marked by their orderliness.

If bureaucracy was what America wanted, Jones was the man to administer it.

In the spring of '41, Jones' man, Emil Schram, chairman of the RFC, was lined up for a $25,000-a-year job as governor of the Chicago Reserve Bank. Eccles petulantly vetoed it on the ground that he had not been consulted. A few weeks later Schram was named president of the New York Stock Exchange at a reputed salary of $48,000 a year.

In bandying his stabilization fund around, Morgenthau trespassed upon Jones' Export-Import bank, which lends money to foreign countries. The first thing he knew, Jones had taken over Morgenthau's business of liquidating British holdings in this country.

Morgenthau promised, when the question of the seven-billion lend-lease bill was pending before the Senate, that he was arranging that British nationals had to liquidate all of their investments in this country as a condition for getting the seven billions. He had just worked out one liquidation when Jones stepped in and loaned the British-owned Brown and Williamson Tobacco Corporation of Louisville $40,000,000. The money went to the parent company in Britain and then was sequestered by the British government. The difference between this and Morgenthau's liquidating operations was that the Louisville firm made enough money eventually to repay the loan, and the property would revert to the British owners. Thereafter, Jones took over the liquidation of British-owned securities in this country. Several months later, in October, Morgenthau moved to take over the borrowing power of Jones' agencies.

CHAPTER VIII

Conflict in the Supreme Court

THIS country's founding fathers, in setting up a "democracy," sought to get away from kingships and royal families, but with an eye to permanence of government they created the Supreme Court. Administrations came and administrations went, but a continuing umpire in the affairs of men was the nation's highest court, as far removed from the conflict of life as it was possible to make a body of mortal men. They were given security, and in the nature of things they came to be an elderly group of dispassionate, philosophical minds. Down over the years the court was to serve as the symbol of a country's essential unity despite its political revolutions.

Even Mussolini thought it wise to maintain the throne as the symbol of government. The sorely tax-burdened British pay millions of pounds a year for the upkeep of a throne which exercises no authority over their lives. It was a tremendous letdown to them and played no small part in the weakness with which they first confronted Hitler, when Windsor, forsaking his responsibility, gave up his throne.

But in Washington, in the summer of 1941, the Supreme Court had ceased to hold the place it had long exercised in government. Not only this, it had lost its detached position as umpire. It had lost its aloofness from political conflict. Figuratively, it was engaging in the street brawls, the contentions of the countinghouse, and the gossip of the cocktail parties. This symbolized, if it was not largely responsible for, the degeneration of official Washington that seemed to be taking place.

After Justice Harlan F. Stone became Chief Justice in June, he confided to some friends that he hoped to get the members of the court out of controversy and conflict and to confine their activities to the court and thus recover the dignity of their office.

His first problem was to be Felix Frankfurter.

Washington's impression of Frankfurter's activity in matters which should not have been his concern was satirized at a spring dinner of the famous Gridiron Club. Frankfurter was so put out by the skit that he jumped up from his place at the head table and rushed over and whispered excitedly in Roosevelt's ear. The President nodded his head gravely. Ordinarily, he would possibly have laughed, but he knows Frankfurter is very sensitive.

Frankfurter's elevation to the bench didn't stop him from moving in and out of the White House to advise with Roosevelt. Indeed, up until the late spring he gave secret audiences to young Joe Alsop, who until he joined the Navy in June was one of Washington's most controversial syndicated columnists and an effec-

tive vehicle for one group of New Dealers. The "behind-the-scenes" columnists have to have authoritative
contacts, and to have these contacts the columnist naturally has to play their game. It is difficult for him to
know, when he is being told what the President is
thinking or intending to do, for example, whether this
is true or whether it is what his informant wants the
President to be thinking or intending to do. The contact has to come through with enough worthwhile information, of course, to retain the columnist's interest.

The New Dealers were past masters at making columnists their vehicles in this way. The amazing career
of Tommy Corcoran in the New Deal was in no small
degree due to his ability properly to space real information with his own propaganda in the columns. Alsop,
who was still in his twenties, was unusually impression-
able. He was a brilliant writer but inexperienced in
Washington. He was a graduate of Harvard and related to the Roosevelts on the Eleanor and Alice side.
When he first came to Washington, Alice was an influence with him. Then he switched to Cousin Eleanor.

Under Frankfurter's wing, Alsop launched a crusade
for intervention which was the talk of small-townish
Washington. Frankfurter purported to tell him what
was going on in the President's mind. Whether it was
what Frankfurter wanted to go on, was a serious question. Day after day, the President was represented as
being in a terrible dilemma. He knew that Britain was
just about to go under, yet he couldn't bring this country to a realization of the seriousness of the situation.

He was just waiting for an incident, the Frankfurter-Alsop team reported.

On June 9, Alsop appeared with a story which set the isolationists in Congress on their ears. While Mr. Roosevelt had been supposedly waiting for the "incident," he reported, the "incident" had already occurred; not just one incident, but two incidents. The column reflected an impatience as to why Mr. Roosevelt didn't act.

"In one case, rather more than a month ago," the column reported, "an encounter between German and American warcraft at sea very nearly terminated in an attack by the Germans. In another, slightly more recent, an attack on what was believed to be a German submarine was actually made by an American destroyer."

Alsop's newspaper colleagues and Senators believed that Secretary of the Navy Knox, who was champing at the intervention bit, was responsible for this particular story, rather than Frankfurter. It developed that Alsop had a week previously been commissioned in the Naval Intelligence Reserve and a few days after the story appeared he was called to active duty and given a confidential assignment in India. Knox was called before a secret session of the Senate Naval Affairs Committee.

Knox insisted that the first "incident" did not occur. Concerning the second, he said an American destroyer was engaged in rescuing sixty survivors of a torpedoed vessel when the destroyer's operator of the listening equipment reported he thought he heard a submarine.

"The captain immediately turned toward the direction indicated and dropped three depth charges," Knox explained. "In doing this, he very prudently exercised the right of self-preservation, for had the submarine been there, his destroyer might have been sunk. There was no other evidence that a submarine was there, and it is quite possible no submarine was there. The listening equipment echo might have been received from a whale or a large fish, or a cold current, instead of a submarine—something which is frequently experienced."

Senator Hiram Johnson of California asked:

"Now, how did these people (Alsop and his associate, Robert E. Kintner) get hold of that?"

Secretary Knox replied:

"I happen to know how they got hold of that, because I went after the fellow with spikes in my boots. As I understand it, it was told to a Boston *Post* reporter on the streets of Boston by a couple of members of the crew of the destroyer when she came home."

Senator Brewster of Maine pointed out that Alsop had been sworn in as a Naval Reserve officer, and by Knox personally, a week before this incident was reported in his and Kintner's column.

"What about discipline?" he asked.

"I gave him the most godawful bawling out that a man ever got," Knox replied.

The Senators then developed that since this episode

Alsop had been called to active duty and given a confidential assignment.

"What possible dependence can you place upon a man performing accurately a confidential mission when you have had such experience with him as you have had?" Senator Johnson asked.

"Well, you have to choose," replied Knox. "I gave him hell, all right. You had to choose between a reprimand and a discharge. My judgment may have been in error. I took the former rather than the latter course."

Senator Byrd of Virginia observed:

"What disturbs me about it, Mr. Secretary, very frankly is that you gave him this confidential commission, which must have been of some importance, after this occurrence and after your reprimand to him."

The Pearson and Allen *Merry-go-Round* had reported on June 23 that a group of American naval vessels had just returned from its "first experience at Atlantic 'patrol' or 'convoying.' "

"Whatever it is called," this column reported, "they helped to get about eighty British merchantmen safely most of the way to the West Coast of Africa. Then the British took over."

Knox described this to the committee in secret session as "a perfect piece of fabrication."

Other newspapermen questioning Knox after the publication of these two columns had been unable to get either confirmation or denial from him. The stories remained unchallenged until the Senate committee's investigation on July 29. The whole episode is typical of a phase of the confusion of Washington. At that time Knox, Secretary of War Stimson, and interventionist organizations were hard-pressing Mr. Roosevelt to intervene. Alsop's crusade caused so much controversy in Washington that his draft-board chairman reported he received more inquiries as to Alsop's draft status than he did about any one else. In fact, it was this and the razzing of his colleagues which caused the younger man to drop his column, for which he and Kintner were receiving $30,000 a year, and join up.

Frankfurter lost a vehicle by which he had been contributing considerably to the confusion of Washington, as did Adolph A. Berle, Jr., Assistant Secretary of State.

Although Frankfurter held practically undisputed sway over the New Deal appointees to the court in party line matters, a distinct rivalry grew up between him and Hugo Black in other cases. Black was perhaps more radical than Frankfurter, and had turned out to be one of the hardest-working members of the court. Their fellow justices looked upon them as vying to write the polished decisions of the late Oliver Wendell Holmes. Frankfurter worked hard at being a stylist in the hope that lawyers and historians would long be quoting his nuggets of brilliancy as they did Holmes's. Black, who was sensitive over the criticism of his paucity of legal learning when he was appointed, wanted every opportunity, himself, to turn out polished and learned opinions, although he did not put in so much work on a particular phrase. The result was that in the chambers of the justices a merry tug-of-war went on between them, and when they could justifiably get an issue on a case in which the New Deal was not particularly interested, they eagerly joined it.

Frankfurter's influence and activities spread out over all New Deal Washington, and necessarily added to the confusion because there were already too many cooks spoiling the broth. Since the advent of the New Deal he had been one of its philosophic leaders. With his coming to Washington his leadership became more direct and aggressive. When Tommy Corcoran left the government, Francis Biddle became his first lieutenant and he looked upon the Department of Justice as his particular domain.

He held frequent meetings of his followers which came to be known around Washington as Frankfurter seminars. At one of these meetings the country's broadcasting setup came under discussion—whether it shouldn't be government-owned, whether newspaper publishers should be permitted to own broadcasting stations, and whether the major networks were not pretty much monopolies. Out of this came the order by the Federal Communications Commission in June that NBC divest itself of one of its chains, that block booking of time be abolished by both NBC and CBS, that other changes in the network system be effected. Such actions on the part of government departments as this frightened conservatives and increased their suspicions, justifiably or not, that the New Dealers were using the national emergency to effect reforms. Instead of unity against Hitler, it made for confusion.

It was estimated that Frankfurter, with Corcoran working with him, had placed some 2,000 young lawyers in the sprawling Washington bureaucracy, many of them in key positions, and he considered himself to be their leader.

But Chief Justice Stone was also concerned about the practice of other justices in making speeches on controversial questions. Justices Owen J. Roberts and Stanley Reed addressed pro-British rallies during the summer. Justice W. O. Douglas still figured in New Deal politics. The New Dealers were forever holding before him the bait that he might be Mr. Roosevelt's successor. In this light they frequently circulated stories that Douglas was tired of the relative quietness of the bench and wanted to return to the field of political conflict. It is doubtful if this was true. He confided to a friend when he was elevated to the Supreme Court that he felt pretty much as did Samuel F. B. Morse when he got his first telegraph message through from Baltimore to Washington. The message read:

"What hath God wrought?"

Nobody hit the Old Order harder than "two-fisted, hard-hitting Bill Douglas," as the New Dealer writers described him, but when he got the security of a $20,000-a-year job for life, he preferred that there be no further disestablishment of our society. And if it were not for that uncertain bait of the presidency he would have kept entirely out of the field of controversy and just sauntered along the rest of his days.

Another of Stone's problems was to be the ill-feeling between the most recently appointed justices, Jackson and Frank Murphy. In June, after the resignation of Chief Justice Hughes, Jackson told the President that as much as he aspired to the highest court in the land, he would not sit on the bench with Murphy. The President explained that as "Chief Justice" Jackson would sit in the middle and preside over the court. Jackson understood until three days before his appointment was announced that he would be Chief Justice instead of just a justice. At the last minute, the President was persuaded that Justice Stone's elevation to the chief justiceship would be decidedly popular, both among liberals and among conservatives. This was done, and Jackson swallowed his feeling against Murphy and joined him on the court.

The latter, an ascetic, came to Washington as Attorney General in January 1939, feeling the bitter sting of the widespread criticism of his handling of the Michigan sit-down strikes in 1937. He had been defeated in November 1938 in his effort to be re-elected as Michigan's governor. A bachelor, he made few friends among the Washington newspapermen. Instead, he looked upon them with suspicion, feeling that they were unsympathetic to the problem which confronted him in Michigan. But to the newspaperwomen he devoted considerable time, explaining that had he not acted the way he did, "another civil war would have occurred." The women, in turn, sought to do missionary work among their men colleagues, insisting that they did not understand Murphy. Most of these men admitted that they didn't.

Less then ten years ago, Murphy, then mayor of Detroit but relatively unknown in national politics, confided in a newspaperwoman:

"I shall be President of the United States."

The newspapermen to whom she passed on the story hooted.

But Murphy, it developed, had not so greatly overstated his reach. A few months after Mr. Roosevelt came into power, Murphy appointed Mrs. Roosevelt's brother, Hall, controller of Detroit. In 1935 Mr. Roosevelt appointed Murphy as governor-general of the Philippines, a job paying $17,000 a year and carrying a mansion and other perquisites. It was at the President's request that Murphy returned to this country to run for governor of Michigan in 1936. The sit-down strikes in the automobile and power industries were called immediately after he assumed office, and Hopkins' WPA supported the strikers' families. Murphy told the Washington newspaperwomen that although he had been greatly misunderstood he felt that under the circumstances it was up to him to make an unusually good record as Attorney General. Thus it was that he kept steadily in the headlines by well-spaced attacks upon corrupt political machines—the Hague machine in Jersey City, the Kelly-Nash machine in Chicago, the old Huey Long gang in Louisiana. He announced an attack against the Crump machine in Memphis, Tennessee, and an attack against alleged gambling and political rackets at Miami and Palm Beach.

When in January 1940 he was appointed to the Supreme Court with Jackson succeeding him, he said wearily that he wished he didn't have to leave his unfinished business. He harped upon this theme for several days and then announced flatly that he had asked the President to defer his appointment so he could insure the carrying out of the crusades he had outlined. This was such a plain reflection upon Jackson that he, already seething with anger, went to the President and demanded that Murphy apologize. Murphy then issued a formal statement saying his investigations had revealed no wrongdoing in Jersey City, Chicago, Louisiana, Memphis or Miami or Palm Beach, and that those cases were closed. Jackson had pointed out to the President that manifestly he wasn't going to pursue a war against the Kelly-Nash and Hague organizations in the face of the impending elections, and it is a fact that they went down the line for the New Deal in those elections.

His explanatory statement issued, Murphy took the oath for the Supreme Court, then hied himself off to Palm Beach for what was described as a much-needed rest, and the eastern rotogravures presently portrayed him basking in a colorful bathing suit on the sands with Palm Beach socialites. The Gridiron spring dinner caricatured him as The Man on the Flying Trapeze. Hughes' usually benign countenance turned purple, Justices Stone and Reed started to laugh, but, feeling the dignity of their office, restrained themselves. Widespread reports persisted about that time—so strongly that Hughes took the unusual step of issuing a formal denial—that the Chief Justice had called Murphy back to Washington and severely lectured him on his lack of dignity.

Now, to add to the Washington confusion in the summer of 1941, Mr. Roosevelt was trying to entice Murphy off the court by telling him he needed him elsewhere, back in the Philippines or as Attorney General. Murphy was unhappy in the court because his legal training was not enough for him to carry his part of the load, and he felt alone; but he was reluctant to leave its emoluments. While other members of the court were out making speeches, Murphy stuck fairly close to Washington during the summer and not infrequently could be seen in the cool of the evenings on the promenades attired in tan and white shoes, linen trousers and odd coat—and hatless—his arm linked with a young girl, sometimes twenty-five years his junior, and talking vigorously. He neither smokes nor drinks, but he freely opens his mind to young women, though he has said he has no intention of marrying. But he did go to Atlantic City to urge the Knights of Columbus to support Britain, and in a closed meeting of this convention he sought to reassure the Catholics on what many of them had considered to be the New Deal's friendship for communism.

Still adding to the confusion of Washington was the bitter conflict between Thurman Arnold, the Department of Justice's famed trust-buster, and the New Dealers, of whom he had ceased to be one.

When Henderson, after his appointment as price czar, announced his broad plans for controlling prices through agreements on the part of industry, he was promptly challenged by Arnold.

In the earlier New Deal days, when industry was being codified, Ickes, then serving his first round as fuel administrator, worked out price and production agreements among the oil companies. Subsequently, the oil companies were prosecuted. Arnold intimated now that he would prosecute any agreements worked out with Henderson. The latter had no statutory law to work under. His job had simply been created by executive order of the President. On the statute books as the law of the land were anti-trust laws, and Arnold contended it was his job to enforce them.

For a period of several weeks cocktail parties enjoyed seeing Henderson and Arnold over in one corner of the room arguing heatedly and shaking their fists at each other. Bob Jackson, who had succeeded Frank Murphy as Attorney General and was yet to get to the Supreme Court, sided with Henderson and in a formal letter to him said the anti-trust laws would be used as a lever over industry to make it co-operate with Henderson. In other words, suits which Arnold was then pressing or about to press would be held in abeyance over industries which played ball and pursued against those which did not. It gave Henderson his first basis on which to operate.

But it put the unorthodox Arnold's career on the shelf temporarily, at least, much to the delight of all the New Dealers but not of the some 300 ambitious young men he had working under him. As a result they kept up a running fight against their fellows, but in return the latter, led by no lesser personage than Felix Frankfurter, pressed hard to run Arnold out of town. Arnold had committed the unforgivable sin of seeking to apply the anti-trust laws to labor organizations, practically on the eve of the 1940 campaign, and had been at outs with the New Dealers ever since.

The New Dealers hit upon an anti-trust crusade during the Christmas holidays in 1937 as a means of diverting attention from the so-called recession of that year. The anti-trust laws have long been enacted, but their enforcement has been a matter of taste with succeeding administrations. Jackson, then Assistant Attorney General, conceived an enforcement crusade on the basis of the thesis which Henderson had prepared for Hopkins and the President to show that the high price of steel was responsible for the recession. And Jackson and Ickes together launched it with a blistering radio attack on industry on a night when the needles were just beginning to fall off the Christmas trees. A few months later, Jackson was promoted to Solicitor General, and somebody else—a colorful character—had to be brought in to carry on the crusade. Arnold, a law

professor at Yale who had been augmenting his income
by doing odd chores for the New Deal, was selected
and widely advertised after the fashion of a radio come-
dian or an actress. The New Dealers had a way of building up their personalities as a business launches a new
product or the movie producers a new star. They "talk
them up" in the Washington propaganda mill.

In the following weeks—he took office in March 1938
—Arnold's name swept across the nation's headlines
with even greater flare than Mr. Roosevelt's or J. Edgar
Hoover's. Day after day the newspapers bannered his
moving against this malefactor or that. He rapidly
came into great demand at cocktail parties, where his
aptitude for saying the first thing that entered his mind
—in rare intellectual phraseology—labeled him as a
genius. He was the celebrity of the hour.

But the anti-trust enthusiasm of the New Dealers
was short-lived. It had served its agitation purposes in
a few months, and they decided, with unusual sudden-
ness, that it was futile to try to make little businesses
out of big ones. They turned to another form of attack
upon the country's economic setup, and to this end
brought about the creating of the famous Senate monopoly or TNEC investigation, which over a period
of several months was to scare the wits out of the insurance companies.

Arnold, however, would not be diverted. An indi-
vidualist, he was determined not to let his vehicle to
fame be taken from him. The New Dealers began to
call him a "buffoon" and to intimate that he was seek-

ing the presidency. And a wealthy woman friend of the Arnolds did promise to finance him for the high office.

He continued to move like a house afire, and in November 1939 announced that labor organizations came under the anti-trust laws just as well as anybody else. If the New Dealers had had their way then, they would have incarcerated him as a dangerous man to be loose. They had split with John L. Lewis and were working like beavers to make up with the American Federation of Labor. Arnold showed his utter lack of team work by getting an indictment against the carpenters' union and its head, William L. Hutcheson, who is also vice-president of the American Federation of Labor. He also proceeded against other AFL unions. However, the New Dealers won the election, as they say, in spite of Arnold. And early in 1941, Frankfurter definitely put him in his place.

The court got around to passing on the Hutcheson case. In an unusual decision written by Frankfurter it was held that the anti-trust laws did not apply to labor. He cited the Norris-LaGuardia anti-injunction act passed by Congress several years ago, which he helped write, as evidence that Congress didn't want the anti-trust laws to apply to labor.

Students of happenings in Washington perceived that Frankfurter had influenced the decision, and that, aside from following the New Deal's party lines on labor matters, it was aimed particularly at the rambunctious Arnold. The later took it that way. It definitely checked his move against organized labor as well as about half of his career, the other half of which was checked by Henderson.

Of Frankfurter the irate Arnold said:

"The difference between Sutherland (late conservative justice whom New Dealers drove off the court) and Felix, is that Sutherland wore his whiskers outside of his head."

The New Dealers in their effort to reform the court in 1937 contended that the conservatives wrote their own philosophies, in favor of corporations, into the Constitution instead of giving it a judicial interpretation. Sutherland was supposed to be the court's best writer of decisions. Arnold claimed that now Frankfurter was doing the same thing, except that his decisions were against corporations. He contended that Frankfurter in his writings at the time the Norris-LaGuardia Act was passed had expressly stated that it did not exempt labor from the anti-trust laws. Undoubtedly this decision at least gave some encouragement to the subsequent wave of strikes in the defense industries.

It looked as if Arnold's days in Washington were numbered after this set-to, and particularly after Henderson gave him the second wallop. When Jackson's long-cherished ambition to go on the court was realized in the early summer, Arnold naturally had ambitions for his job, but Frankfurter advocated Biddle. It would ordinarily follow that Arnold would succeed Biddle as Solicitor General. But Frankfurter and the New Dealers generally wanted to deny him this. In the ensuing squabble there was a question for several weeks whether, because of the rumpus that had been stirred up, Biddle would get the Attorney Generalship, and if he did whether Arnold could even remain in the department.

For ten weeks the Attorney Generalship of the United States was to remain vacant in a national emergency because of the squabbling and also because Mr. Roosevelt was trying to get Murphy to take the place. Biddle, like "Bill" Bullitt, another Philadelphia wealthy aristocrat, eventually got the job. Washington speculated on how long Arnold could remain under him and also what freedom of activity J. Edgar Hoover and his FBI would have under him. Hoover had previously complained to members of Congress that Biddle restricted him in the interest of Communists.

Arnold had developed considerable influence in Congress and was prepared to give Biddle a fight. In the spring, he went over the head of the President's Budget Bureau and the then Attorney General, Jackson, and got an additional appropriation of $750,000 with which to enforce the anti-trust laws. The fact that he could do this with impunity is an example of the confusion of Washington; another example was the fact that with the money he hired additional young lawyers, but Frankfurter and Henderson left them with little or nothing to do. Arnold, however, contending that failure to apply the anti-trust laws to organized labor constituted one of the greatest bottlenecks in defense production, was lobbying in Congress to have the Frankfurter decision overturned.

When Frankfurter was attracting attention while teaching at Harvard with his unorthodox approach to the student's mind, and Arnold was performing similarly at Yale, they and their families were good friends. They used to go around New England together on week-ends performing before intellectual groups. Douglas, then at Yale, and James M. Landis, who was down from Harvard earlier in the New Deal as chairman of the SEC but who went back, were members of the set. They used to pursue such abstruse philosophic discussions as: What is the meaning of Meaning? Frankfurter and Arnold were both prima donnas and keen rivals for the center of the stage. But they were friendly and their wives would prepare scrambled eggs together on Sunday nights.

Landis and Douglas were primarily responsible for Arnold's getting scattered jobs in the early New Deal and subsequently his becoming trust buster, but Frankfurter gave his approval. Then when he tried to pull Arnold away from his overenthusiastic trust-busting bent, the latter paid him no more attention than he did the rest of the New Dealers. He developed not to be one of the Frankfurter boys.

When the Frankfurters came to Washington to live, with Frankfurter's ascension to the court, Mrs. Arnold promptly invited them to dinner. They accepted, but on the eve of the dinner Mrs. Frankfurter called Mrs.

Arnold to say that Felix was so pressed with business they could not make it. Mrs. Arnold said that was too bad, but that they must all get together soon—next week, perhaps?

Mrs. Frankfurter replied:

"Frances, you had better make it two weeks; no, you had better make it two months. Come to think of it, Frances, you had better make it next year."

CHAPTER IX

The "Good-Neighbor" Muddle

It seems that a pretty definite chart has been prescribed for this country's action when Europe goes to war. First, we move toward Europe, and then Germany, to divert us and handicap our contribution, moves to stir up agitation against us in Latin America. Whereupon it behooves us to go on a Latin American friendship spree with one foot while moving toward Europe with the other.

The chart was so clearly drawn in the last World War that it is surprising it was not followed to the letter this time in the interest of simplification and orderly procedure. But in line with advancing civilization it was augmented to give Washington's sprawling bureaucracy still other agencies and to add to the general confusion.

The ordinary procedure is that followed by France and England with the small Eastern European dictatorships—give them gold. In this manner Carol and his mistress Lupescu were able to live in grand state in Rumania, and in addition to have a fortune salted away in foreign countries for the time when they had to flee. Similarly, millions of gold to the Polish leaders was the price they exacted for challenging Hitler, while for more gold Turkey held to a tenuous neutrality.

So Congress appropriated the gold—one-half billion dollars for Latin America. This was simple, direct, and a following of the chart. But an accompaniment of handling the Latin American situation in the Second World War was Harry Hopkins' desire that young men of inherited wealth become acquainted with the "humanitarian objectives" of the New Deal. So he brought in 34-year-old Nelson A. Rockefeller, son of John D. the Second. Young Rockefeller, in turn, brought in Jock Whitney.

In 1936 the Republicans were confident that they knew the American people had a nostalgia for the old American Way. The Republicans arranged for their national convention at Cleveland in high spirits. For the convention they wanted an outstanding piece of pageantry, something that would appeal to what they thought was the yearning of the people for a return to the "old order." They called in the country's leading advertising experts, who were supposed to be past masters in psychology. In what outstanding way, the Republicans asked, could they dramatize this yearning? The advertising experts took the question under consideration. Naturally such a poser as this required study and research and could not be passed upon in a moment.

A good two weeks later one firm submitted an idea that had the appearance of being a knockout, and it was to cost only $100,000. The idea, which came near to sweeping the Republican arrangements committee off its feet, was that the country's oldest living Republican be seated on the platform at Cleveland to symbolize the ruggedness of America. Well, who was this oldest living Republican, the enthusiastic committeemen asked.

"Well, gentlemen," the advertising firm's representative replied in mild reproof, "we can only give you the idea. You'll have to dig up the person yourself."

At that moment one of the committeemen, Clarence Hamlin of Colorado, piped up and said:

"I'll tell you who the oldest living Republican is. He's John D. Rockefeller Senior. Is that the man you want sitting up there on the stage?"

In horror, the other committeemen chorused that it was not.

But Hopkins considered it was worth a considerable sum of money to get John D.'s grandson in with the New Deal. He was set up as Co-ordinator of Commercial and Cultural Relations Between the American Republics, and rapidly built up a staff of 250. He was given $13,000,000 to spend. For several years the State Department had had a Latin American cultural relations branch with annual appropriations of around $750,000, and the business of allotting the half billion dollars was in the hands of the Export-Import Bank, one of the many agencies under Jesse Jones. Also, for years there had been maintained the Pan-American Union, the Bureau of Foreign and Domestic Commerce, and some twenty other agencies dealing with Latin America.

After the Armistice in the First World War the word went around among the A.E.F. that if they did not want to come home immediately, the greatest junket they could get in on was Herbert Hoover's Food Administration. Adventurous young men who wanted to see more of Europe could find very attractive jobs under Hoover in almost any part of Europe they wanted to go to.

The word around Washington in the summer of 1941 was that young Nelson Rockefeller's cultural relations activities were the counterpart of Hoover's food agency, though not operated on anything like as extensive a basis as the Hoover project, which was to form the backbone of his presidential campaign. Not being as widespread as the famous American Relief Administration, which gave away more than $100,000,-000 in post-war Europe, young Rockefeller's enterprise was pretty well confined to college professors and similar "experts." It was not open to the rank and file as was the A.R.A. For one thing, there was not the emphasis then on professors and intellectuals in government that the New Deal was to bring about.

Young Rockefeller's vim and vigor—and he showed plenty of ability—stepped on toes all over official Washington. Development of good relations with Latin

America had been Sumner Welles' ambition ever since he graduated from Groton and embarked upon a career in the diplomatic service during the latter part of Woodrow Wilson's regime.

Before he left the service in Coolidge's administration he had come to be head of the Latin American bureau in the State Department. He was a close friend of the Roosevelts, having as a young man attended their wedding. So he was right at Mr. Roosevelt's side in the interim of the latter's election and inauguration in the winter of 1932–33. He was present when Mr. Roosevelt was having his conferences with Mr. Hoover on the latter's plea that the new President support his foreign policy.

Welles knew he was to be in the State Department— at first as Assistant Secretary of State—before Cordell Hull knew he was to be the Secretary. Welles wished very much to carry out his ideas on Latin America. He was an isolationist and believed that America's foreign policy should center around hemisphere defense. This was Mr. Roosevelt's policy until some time after his re-election in 1936.

The various good-neighbor Pan-American conferences of the Roosevelt administration were largely originated by Welles, and he had brought about the establishment of a bureau to work particularly on cultural relations for which he could never get more than the $750,000 annual appropriation. It can be imagined, then, how he felt when young Rockefeller was brought in and given $13,000,000. In every Latin American country the latter set up offices with directors receiving $8,000 or $9,000 a year. Just as he rubbed Welles the wrong way in Washington, these directors crossed the ambassadors, ministers and consular agents in Latin America. It was no more than human nature that these men should resent what they considered a trespass upon their jobs. For example, young Rockefeller was given $450,000 for an "analysis of totalitarian propaganda" in Latin America. The established embassies and consulates considered this to be just what they were already doing. Certainly it came within their purview. He also had appropriations to study what kind of United States propaganda was likely to be the most effective, and what effect it was having. He had appropriations to study the archaeology of the southern countries, their flora and fauna, all with a view to bringing about an understanding between the northern and southern peoples. It made the diplomatic career men who had always been struggling for appropriations and who since time immemorial had been reporting on every conceivable phase of the countries to which they were assigned, foam at the mouth.

This young man also had appropriations for the exchange of students between North and South American institutions of learning. Obviously, the Latin American students coming to this country for study could not be returned to their own countries and develop any such position of leadership as would be helpful to the United States in time to be of service during the war.

Young men of inherited wealth, "wanting to serve

their country," were numerous in Washington's bureaucracy. Young Mr. Rockefeller was decidedly the most expensive acquisition.

One of his most worthy enterprises, seemingly, was to bring Latin American newspapermen and other visitors to this country and give them a tour of the United States. On one occasion, however, a military mission from Bolivia, being entertained in Detroit, demanded blondes. These visitors also charged several dollars' worth of fancy shirts to their hosts.

The distinguished Argentine scholar, Enrique de Guadia, being met in New York by a State Department official with an itinerary already prepared, asked that he be permitted to see Reno. Leon Pearson, expert on Latin America for the Washington *Times-Herald*, related an interview which the visiting representative of the Argentine newspaper, *La Nación*, Alberto Caprile, had with Harlem's Father Divine. Caprile asked Divine to comment on the good-neighbor policy. Divine asked:

"Do you want me to speak as God or as an ordinary American citizen?"

When told to speak as an ordinary citizen, he said:

"Well, I think we ought to stop all this shilly-shally. We ought to just go to each Latin American country and say: 'How much do you want?' And they name a price, and we buy them and take them over. So that's the end of all the trouble."

Young Rockefeller prepared pamphlets for Latin Americans visiting in this country, seeking to give them useful information; he also prepared pamphlets for citizens of this country visiting in Latin America, telling them how to act. Howls from United States diplomats registered on the willing ears of Sumner Welles. In the spring of 1941 Rockefeller sent Douglas Fairbanks to Mexico City as a good-will ambassador. The State Department criticized this, and then when shortly afterwards it developed that Rockefeller was passing out good-will money to pro-Nazi editors, the diplomats hit the ceiling. They had been promising the friendly editors that when the money bags were opened they would be the ones whose palms were crossed with silver. Such protests were made to the President at this time that henceforth young Rockefeller was directed to get the approval of the State Department for any of his projects. But the money was still flowing freely.

Just after the first of the year Mrs. Roosevelt wanted to make a good-will tour of the southern countries. Stately Cordell Hull quickened perceptibly and suggested that inasmuch as she wrote a daily column everywhere she went, there were diplomatic risks involved. Welles definitely talked her out of it. He and Hull had often disagreed. This was one time they saw eye to eye. But she was not to be wholly outdone, and in August had arranged a radio broadcast in this country and Latin America sponsored by Brazilian coffee exporters. For this she received $2,000 a week, and there was little doubt that she would make a good good-will ambassador.

In the meantime, whatever accomplishments young Rockefeller was making were being nullified by other agencies of the government. He put on a campaign to encourage tourist travel in the southern countries on the part of citizens of this country. Vessels engaged in this trade were taken over for shipments to Britain.

Jesse Jones, up to August, had loaned or earmarked more than $200,000,000 of the half-billion-dollar fund to the various countries to erect steel plants and other industries. Because of lack of shipping facilities and the supposed shortage of the necessary materials either for this country or for shipment to Britain, the plants in many instances were left unfinished or even never started.

Instead of adhering to the simple procedure of giving the Latin American countries money and otherwise assisting them in their loss of their normal European markets, together with countering the Nazi propaganda, the World War No. 2 friendship spree had a grandiose origin which meant that it was launched in confusion and was to proceed in confusion.

With the 1940 presidential campaign warming up, and with a wave of propaganda that the Nazis were practically taking over our southern neighbors, Adolph Berle, Jr., Assistant Secretary of State, a lone wolf among New Dealers in that reference to him as being "brilliant" griped the other "brilliants," was charged with concocting some sort of scheme, a counter stroke designed more for its effect in this country's political campaign than in the countries to the south. He labored at length and produced a long-range program, not one just confined to the war, but one by which Hitler would never be able to get anything from Latin America regardless of how the war came out. Under this program this country would simply buy up, outbidding Hitler, all the exportable products of the twenty-one countries. This was to be done notwithstanding that we have a surplus of those products, except a few such commodities as coffee and war minerals. In normal times Europe takes 50 per cent of these exports and we take only 21 per cent. Similarly 50 per cent of Latin America's imports come from Europe and only 25 per cent from the United States. Thus it can be seen that we were to undertake a job of tremendous magnitude.

Berle was so resented by those New Dealers who were led by Tommy Corcoran before the latter left the government, that they circulated a story that Berle enjoyed his greatest brilliancy while taking a bath, so his wife, in order to be near him on these occasions, had built an adjoining bathtub. They even "planted" this story in a syndicated column so that it appeared in newspapers throughout the country.

His proposal for economic warfare on Hitler met with such derision in Congress that it was whittled down to the half-billion-dollar fund given to Jesse Jones. However, under the provisions of the appropriation it was still possible to go into Berle's plan.

Jones was looked upon by Congress as the assurance that it would not be done.

Nevertheless, a suspicion lurked in Congress that some such plan as this might be broached later in connection with the "Four Freedoms" which Mr. Roosevelt had enunciated. The suspicion persisted that the New Deal was planning some kind of economic warfare to be used after the war to insure a New Deal peace over the world.

One broad general policy underlay the government's activities in Latin America: Support the existing governments as long as they co-operated with us. This meant loans from Jesse Jones' half-billion-dollar fund, or better still, money from the lend-lease fund. It meant entertaining their officials when they came to this country. Secondary enterprises were young Nelson Rockefeller's introduction of Latin American dancers on Broadway and many kindred ways of showing the southern "neighbors" that we were not a high-handed people but very democratic, indeed.

The evidence was overwhelming, however, that our many officials dealing with the situation were inextricably caught in their own propaganda which they used to get increased appropriations and to heighten the war atmosphere. Frequent newspaper headlines emanated from them to the effect that "Nazis Create Powder Barrel Situation in Latin America," or "Nazis Responsible for Ecuador-Peru Clash," or "Bolivian Government Puts Down Nazi Putsch." These were oversimplifications, as everyone with any realistic knowledge of Latin America knew.

The facts were, that Latin America's normal commerce with Europe had been cut into deeply by the British blockade. An even deeper cut was made when we passed the lend-lease bill and Britain, which had shown a preference for Latin American raw materials, turned to us for everything she could get because we were underwriting it. Then, when we declared an embargo on Japan and closed the Panama Canal to her, this cut further into the Latin American trade. So it was with no sudden love for the "Colossus of the North" or any response to the "good-neighbor" policy that the stricken countries turned to North America for succor.

Yet young Rockefeller excitedly related to a secret meeting of the House Appropriations Committee in the late spring how the Germans had twice broken through the British blockade of Brazil and this had given Nazi influence a profound boost over all Latin America. Two German ships entering a Brazilian port after many months had more of an effect on the confusion of Washington than in Latin America. Usually well-informed commentators of Washington getting their "information" from the various officials were wont to write frequently that the South American governments were on the fence watching to see just which way the war would go. If Latin America became convinced that Hitler was going to win, then they would go with him. Under the circumstances, they wrote, it was utterly essential, with a view to preserving hemisphere defense, that our government never leave any doubt in the Southerners' minds as to how the war would come out. Nonsense! Latin America wanted to resume its normal trade, and more likely was concerned not so much as to how the war ended, as when.

There were some 2,500,000 Germans in the ten South American countries and some 6,000,000 Italians; or rather so many people of German and Italian origin, just as we have millions of people of German and Italian origin in this country. They are people who left Europe for the same reasons as the Germans and Italians who came to this country. They are people or the children of people who sought escape from the compressed existence of Europe. Nearly all those of German origin are settled in Brazil—2,000,000 of them. This settlement goes back to 1820. In no single decade between 1887 and 1926 did this immigration exceed 63,000, and after 1926 it had dropped to 3,000 a year. These Germans have largely settled on small farms in the states of Paraná, Santa Catarina and Río Grande do Sul.

The largest Italian populations are in Argentina and Brazil—about 3,000,000 in each country. The Italian migration also goes back to 1820. Between 1820 and 1920 some 1,500,000 settled in Brazil. The earlier Italian immigrants went in for the coffee plantations and the development of vineyards. They have spread out more than the Germans, however, because, like the

Portuguese and the Spanish, who predominate in South America, they are Latins. They have intermarried with the Portuguese and the Spanish and provided many of the leaders of the country.

So far as South America, as distinguished from Central America, is concerned, our friendship spree began with the classification of the most influential and dependable people as subversive influences. Unquestionably, Nazi agents were operating and finding a fertile soil on which to operate. The South Americans were getting plenty of pro-Hitler propaganda, in fact, not only from Nazi agents but from the United States, about how we intended to starve their kinspeople in Europe, and about how, even after the war, we were going to take over the natural trade which they had enjoyed. Unquestionably the various governments were having trouble remaining in power, but this was due far more to economic conditions brought about by the war than to the work of Nazi agents. It didn't take Nazi agents to overthrow Herbert Hoover and bring the New Deal to power in this country in depression times.

Mr. Rockefeller told something about the chaos that was being created when he appeared before the secret session of the House Appropriations Committee. He recalled the half-billion-dollar fund made available for loans and said:

"The government moved into action, starting out with substantial loans to countries that were in difficult financial situations as the result of losses of foreign exchange. We (Mr. Rockefeller's agency) worked with

the Export-Import Bank (Jesse Jones' agency) in preparing basic material for them and co-ordinating our
program with that of the State and other departments,
getting them the figures and advising with them on
minimum import requirements so that they could figure the deficiency of their exchange available for those
imports, and then the loans were made. As you know,
loans totaling around $130,000,000 are outstanding
today. [This was in June.]

"Next we worked on the problem of increasing the
imports to the United States from the other American
countries to compensate for the loss of these European
markets which had, as I have said, severely affected
their internal economies.

"The President wrote a letter to all the depart-
mental heads stating that in the event that purchases
of strategic or critical materials were necessary over
and above the quantities available in the United States
for the defense program, the other American republics
should be given preference in the purchase of those
materials. That resulted in a tremendous increase in
the purchases of copper, nitrates, manganese, tin, and
various other ores, as well as purchases by private consumers of wool and hides plus increased purchases by
private consumers of materials which had come from
Central Europe in the past.

"The situation by this spring was beginning to look
a little better. Adjustments had been made to the war
economy in Europe. The Argentine, it is true, was still
suffering very seriously because of tremendous surpluses

in products that are competitive with our own. We could not take them and the European purchasers were completely shut off. England's purchases were falling off, and they were in a particularly unfortunate position. However, most of the other countries had stabilized their exchange positions, and a great many of the important surpluses had been whittled down. The situation was beginning to look a little better. As a matter of fact, by the first quarter of the present year, the Central and South American countries had a favorable exchange balance with the United States for the first time in some time, which aided them in the purchase of needed materials which they could not produce domestically.

"However, just as the situation seemed to show definite signs of improvement, two new factors have come in very recently. One is the lack of shipping. This is due to the program of the Army and the Navy, coupled with the aid-to-Britain program. Ships operating to the other Americas have been withdrawn and service curtailed seriously; this shipping is the life line of the other American republics because the States are the only place from which they can now purchase iron and steel products, manufactured and semi-fabricated goods.

"On top of that we have a very serious situation which is growing worse every day due to the fact that our industries are working to capacity on defense orders and on increased consumers' demands, with the result that there is a tendency on the part of our companies to lose interest in the filling of orders in Central and South America; as a consequence, these countries are today having an extremely difficult time in getting goods necessary to meet their essential requirements.

". . . We now have a situation down there where industry is stagnating to an increasing degree. You have construction jobs being stopped. In the airplane end of it, at one time there were seventeen unfilled orders in for parts of planes—I think only two of them included new planes—for the maintenance of American equipment which had been sold to these countries. The orders were coming up here for small quantities, ten thousand or twenty thousand dollars of equipment, and there was no interest at all because we needed everything we could get for our own aviation here. As a consequence, in some cases export licenses were refused, or the Army or Navy refused to give permits where the manufacturers were ready to supply the needed articles. The result was that some local air line equipment and even some of the Army and Navy planes of these countries were being grounded because we would not take the trouble to supply the necessary parts."

Mr. Rockefeller did not tell of an incident that occurred just a few days before he gave his recital.

Miss Alvira Vargas, the daughter of the President of Brazil, was flown to this country by Clipper to christen a new liner, the *Rio de Janeiro,* which had been built for the South American trade. Considerable fanfare about Pan-American unity attended the occasion.

Speakers told glowingly of the lasting friendship between this country and her southern "neighbors." Miss Vargas was given the usual diamond necklace which shipowners bestow upon the fair women who christen their ships. Then before she could get back to Brazil the U. S. Navy stepped in and commandeered the vessel.

One of the many agencies dealing with Latin America was the Office of the Administrator of Export Control, with an appropriation of $1,000,000 for the year and some 500 employees. Brigadier General R. L. Maxwell was in charge. He managed to keep out of the limelight through the months of bickering between those charged with Latin American affairs, until in mid-August the New Dealers began hammering at him as the main "bottleneck." He wouldn't grant export licenses for goods for Latin America speedily enough, it was contended.

It was to bring some order out of the chaos in this phase of Washington's confusion, that Mr. Roosevelt just before leaving for his meeting with Winston Churchill set up a Supreme Economic Council headed by Vice-President Henry A. Wallace. As soon as Wallace got organized a few weeks later, he removed Maxwell and sent him back to the Army.

It was characteristic of the confusion of Washington that a debate proceeded for several days—among columnists, editors, Washington correspondents, and in the cloakrooms of Congress—as to just what the new agency was to do. It was called the Supreme Economic Council, or another SEC, which in the Washington alphabet lingo confused it with the Securities and Exchange Commission. The order creating it laid emphasis on the rather indefinable undertaking of conducting economic war, or of "co-ordinating" (co-ordinating was a much-abused term in Washington) our economic operations in Latin America, against Japan, and the lend-lease support of friends of the democracies.

Some such setup had been in the making for several months, according to the Washington rumor factory, and Secretaries Hull and Morgenthau, and Jesse Jones and Leon Henderson had all been seeking to get control of it. Hull wanted it to be placed under Dean Acheson, an Assistant Secretary of State; Jones wanted it under his deputy in the Federal Loan Administration, Will Clayton; and Morgenthau wanted it under his Under-Secretary of the Treasury, Herbert Gaston.

But now that the setup had been announced, was its scope to be confined to the "economic warfare" or was it also to be the over-all defense agency? The order creating it permitted this. Mr. Roosevelt had gone to sea, and Wallace left promptly for a vacation in Colorado. As usual, the council was widely ballyhooed by New Deal publicists as one of the most important steps that this government had ever taken. It was described as tantamount to a knockout blow for Hitler. Economic warfare, according to the New Deal publicity, was far more important than guns, bullets, and men.

In the ensuing speculation as to its full scope, the more importance was attached to the council, the more feeling increased in officialdom and Congress against the appointment of Wallace to head it. About two weeks later he was also named chairman of the newly created SPAB.

This former Iowa farm editor was always as much of a mystery to Washington as Frank Murphy in the Supreme Court. There was an air of mysticism about him. He had never run with the Frankfurter or Ickes New Dealers. In a retiring way, always giving the impression of downright timidity, he built up a bureaucracy in the Department of Agriculture that was to top all the other New Deal bureaucracies put together.

His father served as Secretary of Agriculture under Coolidge, and friends of the elder Wallace have insisted that the manner in which Herbert Hoover, as Secretary of Commerce, took one bureau after another from him, hastened his death. At any rate, Hoover's treatment of the father left an indelible impression on the son. Although a lifelong Republican, he supported Al Smith against Hoover in the presidential campaign of 1928. In 1932 he again and more vigorously opposed Hoover and supported Roosevelt. When he was named Secretary of Agriculture his farm paper was bankrupt. In the ensuing years he was to bring about a complete regimentation of American agriculture and to build up a bureaucracy which had some 13,000 employees in Washington alone and more than 200,000 in the field. All the while he professed a weary aversion to "all this power being heaped upon my shoulders." Yet on occasions when Congress showed a disposition not to heap any more on him, he would become as hard as steel, and before his opponents knew what was happening, he had gotten the additional power.

Mr. Roosevelt's selection of him to be his vice-presidential running mate was the sensation of the 1940 Democratic convention at Chicago. It was a crushing blow to at least ten other aspirants. And it enraged the Southern delegates and Ickes as well as Paul Mc-Nutt and the former Assistant Secretary of War, Louis Johnson. The resentment was so widespread in the convention, in fact, that had the rival contenders for the honor been able to pool their strength Mr. Roosevelt would have been soundly defeated.

In the campaign that followed, Wallace threw his traditional isolationism to the winds, and crusaded with an evangelical fervor for the crushing of Hitler. He high-noted the charge of "appeaser" which the New Dealers leveled at Willkie. In the First World War, Willkie served in France. Wallace got exemption from military service on the grounds that his farm paper was an essential service.

In the presidential campaign, the newspapers published by the late Paul Block dug up an exchange of correspondence which he had purportedly carried on over a period of several months with the woman leader of an unusual religious cult in Brooklyn. The organization got into financial difficulties during the depression and she came to Washington seeking relief for it. She met Wallace and he became very much interested in the teachings of the cult, according to the correspondence. In the correspondence, Wallace carried on a frank discussion of his aims in life, his beliefs about the hereafter, and the aims of the New Deal. Frequent reference was made to the Lama of Tibet. Mr. Roosevelt was frequently referred to by Wallace as "The Flaming One."

The Paul Block newspapers called in handwriting experts, and they were convinced of the authenticity of Wallace's signature. Their star reporter, Ray Sprigle, was sent to the Middle West to get comment from Wallace on the letters. He subsequently reported to his office that Wallace evaded him through several states, but that eventually he accosted him just as Wallace was rushing through the station to take a train. As soon as he identified himself, he reported, Wallace reached into his pocket and handed Sprigle a statement, already prepared, denying any knowledge of the letters. Two other publishers, supporting Willkie in the campaign, pleaded with Block not to publish the letters. They contended that Willkie had the campaign won and that the publication of the letters might be a boomerang. A few weeks before Block died he related to some of his friends that of all the mistakes he had made in life, he considered the failure to publish these letters a major one.

But the existence of the letters was widely known to Senators and in Washington official circles, and it influenced their impression of Wallace. That the President would continue to place him in important positions of government adversely influenced them in their attitude toward Mr. Roosevelt. It muddled their thinking in times of a national emergency, made them distrustful. This added to the confusion of Washington.

Wallace and Ickes had been fighting for years in particular over Ickes' efforts to get the Bureau of Forestry from the Department of Agriculture to Ickes' Interior Department. The former's appointment revived the New Dealers' story of early 1940, to the effect that Mr. Roosevelt was only running for the third term because of the international situation, and that as soon as Hitler was crushed he planned to resign. Was he now bringing Wallace forward as the heir apparent?

It was typical of the confusion in Washington in the summer of 1941 that questions of this sort motivated men; in some instances, it utterly dominated their thinking.

Aside from the confusion attendant upon the creation of the Wallace Economic Council, the government's whole policy of short-range economic warfare against the Axis powers was wrapped in bickering and confusion.

Ever since Japan joined the Axis, Ickes had conducted a crusade in the President's cabinet for an embargo on all exports to that country. He carried on his crusade by telling of cabinet deliberations to columnist friends. On one occasion, in 1939, Mr. Roosevelt, as an example of how closely he read the newspapers, observed to an aide:

"I see Harold has quit telling the columnists about what goes on in the cabinet meetings."

But this was just because he had not been able to put his finger on any of Ickes' work recently. Ickes hadn't quit.

Cordell Hull and Sumner Welles, being charged with the conduct of the nation's foreign affairs and acting on the basis of information they received from our diplomatic representatives all over the world, insisted upon pursuing a policy, as they explained it and as Mr. Roosevelt once explained it, of letting Japan have enough oil and other material to keep her from, in sheer desperation, moving against the Dutch East Indies. An embargo on scrap iron was suggested by two Republican Senators, Vandenberg of Michigan and Styles Bridges of New Hampshire, before the outbreak of war in Europe in 1939, and it was finally applied in August 1940, though exports were still permitted from Latin America. Even after economic warfare was declared by the administration in July 1941, Hull and Welles continued to try to wean Japan from the Axis with a view to our not having trouble on two fronts, and Ickes, who was not in a weaning-away mood, sought to hamstring them by telling the columnists of their negotiations and representing them as "appeasers." Thus the nation's foreign policy was being conducted in the same backbiting and confusion that pervaded the rest of official Washington. Ickes was constantly sharpshooting at Hull and Welles to force our seizing Martinique for the oil tankers said to be there. It was not a matter of the marines just moving in and taking the island. Georges Roberts, the French high commissioner of Martinique, jovially assured visiting American newspapermen while he served a rum cocktail of which he was proud, that there would be a "good fight" before the island was taken. Similarly, Ickes pressed for the seizure of Dakar. At times, in the cabinet sessions, he had Knox, Stimson and Morgenthau with him; the former two more than the latter.

With the passage of the lend-lease bill in March, China was embraced as part of our crusade for democracy, and $50,000,000 allocated to her. Ickes renewed his demand for a complete embargo against Japan. Our government was then in the paradoxical position of giving China material with which to fight Japan and in turn letting Japan have the material with which to fight China. This seemed to be an untenable position, but it was adhered to for several months.

In the meantime, one of Mr. Roosevelt's anonymous aides, Lauchlin Currie, was sent to China ostensibly to study its budget and apply the lend-lease allocation. Currie was referred to by the New Dealers as one of their ace "brilliants." Invariably the publicity concerning him emphasized his passion for anonymity, yet he had three scrapbooks filled with newspaper and magazine clippings in his office. He was born in Nova Scotia in 1903. He attended the London School of Economics and came under the influence of John Maynard Keynes. Currie was instrumental in Keynes' getting entrée to the White House. Currie himself was brought down from Harvard, where he was teaching on money and banking early in the New Deal, and came to be referred to as Marriner Eccles' one-man "brain trust" in the Federal Reserve Board.

He became one of Mr. Roosevelt's trusted advisers early in the year. His trip to China did not arouse any unusual attention until his return, when reports were circulated that his conferences with the Chinese leader, Chiang-Kai-shek, had as much to do with establishing the New Deal's "Four Freedoms" in China as with administration of the lend-lease fund. He was reported to have brought Chiang to a wholesale reorganization of his government, and to acceptance, at least in principle, of a Chinese New Deal. This included heavier taxation on the landowners and the siphoning of the additional revenue back to the poor.

So now the direct proposition of financing China in her war with Japan came to be associated with a vague ambition of the New Dealers, which their critics could not exactly define but which irritated them, of "New Dealizing" the world. The fact that there were elements in the Washington conglomeration that were convinced, or at least suspicious, that the New Dealers had a much broader program than the crushing of Hitler, was at bottom of much of the confusion.

Ickes, to the increasing anger of Hull and Welles, concentrated on his campaign for direct action against Japan. When he became fuel administrator in June, one of his first acts was to order a vessel, loaded with oil for Japan, held up at Philadelphia. This was in direct opposition to the policy of the State Department.

Just how much this act of Ickes, or rather his agitation over a long period, had to do with subsequent events, of course, is not known. We do know, however, that in July, Japanese forces occupied the southern part of Indo-China, and that the United States Government immediately froze all Japanese funds in this country and declared an embargo. The newspaper headlines heralded the imminence of war between the two countries.

There is always the question, in matters of this kind, as to which comes first, the egg or the chicken. In the long period of negotiations between our State Department and the Japanese Foreign Office, the Japanese diplomats in Washington were constantly reporting on Ickes' agitation, and attempting to assay the progress he was making with Mr. Roosevelt. There is no way of knowing—when the Japanese did move into southern Indo-China, which in turn, forced the hand of our government—how much they were influenced by the fear that Ickes' will would prevail.

In moving into southern Indo-China the Japanese were 800 miles closer to the British naval base of Singapore than they had been since the autumn of 1940. They had been in the northern portion of this country since then.

K. Kaito, for several years the correspondent in Washington of the Japanese press association, Domei, and who attended the President's and the State Department's press conferences along with the American newspapermen, was highly amused.

"You ask me what happen now, thank you, please," he said in answer to the inquiries of his American colleagues with a wide grin. "I do not know. Whatever happens, we are in a better position—a leetel better than we were. If we have to fight, it is better, yes, yes, thank you please, it is better that we are here than that we are there—do you understand. It is—what do you call it—yes, yes—it is a big poker game—yes, yes, it is a big poker game. Yes, yes, please."

CHAPTER X

Ickes, Oil, and War-Consciousness

In early July, Wendell Willkie lunched with Mr. Roosevelt. These two opponents in one of America's most heated presidential campaigns were together for an hour and a half. They talked about many things, but one had to do with the President's difficulty in making the country war-minded, or in bringing it to a realization of what both Mr. Roosevelt and Mr. Willkie considered the seriousness of the world situation confronting it.

Mr. Roosevelt laughingly remarked to his visitor that some of his friends had suggested he call in the country's leading psychiatrists. To this Willkie demurred, saying he considered no one understood the American mind and how to influence it any better than the President.

Yet the President was here admitting that, notwithstanding his success in the past, he was now falling short in his greatest undertaking. His inability to make the country war-conscious was responsible for much of the confusion that existed in Washington in 1941. It was responsible for exciting utterances

[183]

on the part of subordinates who attempted to do it for him. For example, Ickes, although possessed of a natural yearning to attract attention, when harping insistently upon gasless Sundays, nevertheless had some justification in that this was his contribution to the war psychology campaign. To be made to feel themselves a part of the war, the American people must be brought to sacrifice, to denial of comforts they had hitherto enjoyed.

On the other hand, was it necessary to make the country war-conscious? Mr. Roosevelt had repeatedly said that he was determined to crush Hitler regardless of what that entailed. But not one of his closest intimates knew what he believed it entailed. Did he think that our economic contribution would be sufficient? In that event, making the country hysterical seemed wholly unnecessary and possibly dangerous. Or did he consider that another A.E.F. would be necessary, sooner or later? In that event, manifestly he had considerable work to do in this country. He did not confide in congressional leaders, except to give them pieces of alarming information when he wanted particular legislation; neither did he confide in members of his cabinet. Columnists and other writers variously represented his thinking on the basis of what their informant thought was his thinking or what the informant wanted the thinking to be.

Thus, as he was returning from his historic meeting with Churchill, various of his closer associates urged that his arrival be built up into a tremendous ovation. Wendell Willkie urged Mr. Roosevelt to use his meeting with Churchill as a springboard for a barnstorming tour of the country. So also did the interventionist Fight for Freedom Committee, which carried Senator Carter Glass among its sponsors, but was organized by young Barry Bingham, publisher of the Louisville *Courier-Journal,* as a memorial to his father who had served as ambassador to Great Britain. Whether Mr. Roosevelt disapproved of the "ovation" plan or whether circumstances militated against it, was not known. It did not come off.

The usually mild-mannered Secretary of Agriculture, Mr. Wickard, felt it incumbent upon himself in June to announce the imminence of food shortages—in a country whose farmers for eight years had been paid to curtail their crops. Besides, Britain, from the beginning of the war in Europe, had shown a lack of interest in this country's food supplies. It could get such supplies from South America and its dominions. Back in the fall of 1939, Southern members of Congress together with their Middle-Western brethren had led the fight for the modification of the Neutrality Act which prohibited exports to nations at war, in the conviction that it would prove a great boon to the cotton, wheat, and corn growers.

However, the farmers did not profit. Wickard and his aides in the Agriculture Department, notably Milo J. Perkins, in charge of Surplus Commodities, complained that they were having to shove the food down the throats of the British. With reports of starvation and semi-starvation coming from most of Europe, Congress in the spring of 1941 appropriated a billion or so for benefits to American farmers under a crop-curtailment program, and the Secretary of Agriculture warned of food shortages.

With the passing of the seven-billion-dollar lend-lease bill in March, the British representatives in Washington became more interested in this country's food supplies, inasmuch as we had now obligated ourselves to footing the bill. Previously they had preferred, in order to conserve their cash, to get agricultural products from their dominions and South America. Even the modified neutrality bill provided that all sales had to be on a cash basis.

But one of the most ambitious efforts at making the country war-conscious was that of Mayor Fiorello H. La Guardia of New York, known far and wide over the country as the Little Flower. It should be understood that when a country is suddenly shifted into a war economy it becomes utterly essential for ambitious politicians to become a part of it. If they are to remain as leaders, or in the headlines, they must have an active part, or "leadership" of some kind, in the new set-up. The endeavor with which they have previously occupied the headlines ceases to be of headline nature.

This was the case with La Guardia. An indefatigable, stocky little bundle of energy, he served in Congress as a Socialist and as a Republican, and landed as mayor of the country's largest city, running on the Fusion ticket, with the support of the Republican and American Labor parties. In the presidential campaign of 1940, Mr. Roosevelt was rightfully worried about the Italian vote of New York City. Aside from the fact that Mussolini was a part of the Axis, the President in a speech at Charlottesville, Virginia, earlier in the year, had characterized Mussolini's attack on France as a "stab in the back," which, because of the Italian's predilection for the stiletto, was looked upon as overly appropriate. La Guardia, of Italian vintage, was a leader of the Italians in New York. They constituted a main source of his political strength. So, with a view to mollifying them, Mr. Roosevelt, in a grand flourish of publicity, named La Guardia to head a commission which was to go to Canada and work out a joint defense program between Canada and this country in the event of attack by Hitler. Inasmuch as the military establishments of the country have their files filled with plans to deal with such contingencies, regardless of how remote, it was possible for the mayor to announce after three fleeting visits to Ottawa, that a quite invulnerable scheme had been worked out. The Republicans gritted their teeth, but there was no way they could combat such ingenuity. As it turned out, however, Mr. Roosevelt didn't get the Italian vote after all.

But in the spring of 1941, La Guardia, intending to run in the fall for a third term as mayor, was terribly anxious to get into the Washington picture. He went frequently to see Mr. Roosevelt, and on each occasion let newspapermen get the impression that the President was trying to get him to take over some responsible job in the defense setup, perhaps that of the overall director for which there was considerable agitation through the country. Definitely, he was trying to get the President to bring him into the picture.

There was then functioning in the OPM a Council of Governors by which it was sought to co-ordinate the defense problems of the states with the Federal government. It was directed by Frank Bane, who was the executive director of the Council of Governors with headquarters in Chicago. Paul McNutt, as former governor of Indiana, was very active in this. La Guardia, however, dominated the pressure group known as the Conference of Mayors, whose greatest contribution to the public weal was to get Federal money for municipal projects. La Guardia kept trying to convince the President that there was need of a co-ordinating agency much broader than the OPM, and that he could furnish this through his fellow mayors. There ought to be some activities to make the country war-conscious, he argued, such as test evacuations of populations, blackouts. This struck a responsive chord with Mr. Roosevelt, because he was certainly having trouble making the country war-conscious.

Secretary Ickes had argued on the need of making the country war-conscious when he took the Caribbean trip with Mr. Roosevelt in December. The President upon his return directed his evangelical Vice-

President, Henry A. Wallace, to draw up a plan. Mr. Roosevelt was quite impressed by the religious-like zeal with which Wallace went after the things he wanted. Wallace drew up the plan and presumed he was to carry it out. But he stepped on the toes of Lowell Mellett, the director of Mr. Roosevelt's Office of Government Reports, so the plan was turned over to him.

Mellett, however, did nothing about it—or so Ickes was to complain to columnist friends several months later—and a bitter denunciation against Mellett was printed. Those long and intimately associated with Mellett believed that this former Scripps-Howard editor was perhaps the most intense and sincere of the New Dealers, and that he feared that if this country went to war, Labor's so-called social gains would be engulfed in the turmoil. Whether this was true or not, it was clearly apparent that he was not enthusiastic about war propaganda.

Mellett gave up a very influential position with Scripps-Howard when Roy W. Howard opposed Mr. Roosevelt on the latter's attempt to reform the Supreme Court in 1937. He took a trip around the world, and when he returned, the New Dealers felt grateful and wanted to make room for him in their midst. Mellett did not need a job, as he was comfortably fixed. But by way of bringing him into the set, he was placed at the head of the National Emergency Council. This was something that Mr. Roosevelt created out of a clear sky early in his administration and supported with funds which Congress had voted for relief. It was announced as a co-ordinating agency. Its annual expenditures ranged as high as $1,500,000, and it had one director after another— Donald Richberg, who had served as general counsel for the NRA; Frank Walker, who became Postmaster General after Jim Farley's retirement, and others. It never made any serious attempt, however, at co-ordinating, and was more or less just an agency spending money when Mellett took over.

As was so often the case with men whom Mr. Roosevelt took on and gave titles to, it was up to Mellett to make his job. He did. He turned it into probably the most unusual agency our government has ever had. It was to be the eyes and ears of Mr. Roosevelt. In each state was a director, a man who knew the state from one end to the other. It was his business to keep in touch with the thinking of communities, whether they were satisfied with the WPA project, the NYA operations or the farm allotments, how they felt about war, particularly how they felt about Mr. Roosevelt. These directors made secret reports to Mellett on the conduct, the character, the political faith of the countless Federal appointees and likewise on those whom Senators recommended. Thus a check was kept on the farflung operations of Jesse Jones, of the Department of Agriculture, and the like. If a governor of a state applied for Federal money to carry out a particular project, the director reported confidentially to Mellett on the worthiness of the project and whether the governor was of a kind the New Deal should politically help. The director reported on a young, up-and-coming politician, whether the New Deal should support him in his effort to oust older and less New Dealish politicians.

In the past, Congress had served as the eyes and ears of the President. But now, Congressmen calling on the President to apprise him of a situation in their district, or a state of feeling, were surprised to find him already fully informed, and perhaps at cross purposes with their information. All recent Presidents have had unofficial political scouts, usually political hangers-on, but the reports of the Congressmen prevailed.

Congressional committees and visiting editors frequently questioned Mellett in 1941 over reports that a censorship was to be applied. They were far off the track of Mellett's real function. The appropriation for his office for the fiscal year beginning July 1 was $1,500,000.

Mr. Roosevelt finally set La Guardia up, in mid-June, as director of the Office of Civilian Defense. A palatial Massachusetts Avenue mansion was taken over as offices for his 250 employees, and Congress gave him $900,000 for the fiscal year beginning July 1. He told the House Appropriations Committee in one of its closed sessions that, of course, he would have to come back for an appropriation of several millions as soon as he could prepare estimates on the additional and auxiliary fire equipment that would be needed to fight fires started by bombs. In all of the eastern coastal communities and communities back as far as five miles from the coast, or even in the industrial city of Pittsburgh, he explained, every fire house would need additional equipment costing about $43,000. And he said every fire house should have an auxiliary fire-fighting force five times as large as its present force. It would take a year and a half to get the additional equipment, but in the meantime the auxiliary force could be trained by going to fires with the regular firemen. This additional equipment would further draw from the country's supply of steel and other metals. Some members of the committee could not suppress smiles as the mayor talked about fire-fighting equipment. His great hobby was to go to fires and ride on fire trucks. He had a fireman's helmet in his New York office, and when he heard the siren he could hardly keep his feet still.

But this was to be only one phase of his defense enterprise. Citizens, he said, would have to be trained as fire wardens; buildings in all the communities of the "danger" zone would have to be studied to determine whether it was better for the occupants to stay in or get out in the event of an air raid; committees would have to be set up to get people off the streets because of our natural proclivity for running out to see the excitement; there would have to be first-aid stations, and the like. The mayor had already sent a couple of men over to London to see just exactly how it was done over there.

As soon as he finished his appearance before the committee he caught a plane for New York. Before appearing, however, he had absorbed the OPM's council in his organization and forthwith booted Bane and his aides out.

In the wave of publicity attending his new job, women volunteers about the country, who were to serve under him, got to fighting over a design for their uniforms and whether they should have both dress and working uniforms. The matter apparently assumed such importance that the newspaperwomen in Washington were moved to ask Mrs. Roosevelt about it at one of her press conferences. She said she supposed there should be some distinctive recognition of the women's work, but she expressed cautious doubt that a dress uniform was also needed, and on the various designs that were submitted to her she side-stepped comment.

The governors didn't show a disposition to co-operate with the mayor. They continued to clear their problems through their council at Chicago, and it in turn cleared them through the OPM at Washington. The mayor, with his business of running New York, of watching his campaign for re-election, and giving at least an occasional eye to the joint defense plans of Canada and the United States, could only get down to Washington infrequently. Inasmuch as his fire engines were to be a long time in coming, his staff was hard put to find something to do. To fill this gap, the nation-wide collection of aluminum pots and pans was cooked up. Here was something the Office of Civilian Defense could do. It was not originally created for this, of course, but any war expert knows that unanticipated problems come up in blitzkrieg war times, and that the really worthwhile agency is one that can be adapted to meet them. Robert E. McConnell, head of the conservation department of the OPM, offered to help, as did the Council of Governors. The ensuing campaign to get the housewives to donate aluminum trinkets, kitchenware, anything aluminum—the primary purpose being to make them war-conscious, get them into the necessary spirit of sacrifice—was marked by squabbling among the three agencies. Because of La Guardia's preoccupation with other matters, however, it remained for McConnell and the Council of Governors to achieve such success as was had. And the business of making the country war-conscious, in so far as La Guardia was concerned, had to wait for the outcome of his campaign for re-election in November. But Mrs. Roosevelt joined the OCD in October to pep it up.

Washington would undoubtedly have been in a state of confusion in the summer of 1941 had the only man in the government been Harold Ickes. He is confusion itself. The newspapers of the capital dubbed him "Horrible Harold." But his "war-conscious" campaign was the most heroic of all. In the eight years he had served in the cabinet he had warred, at one time or another, with every one of his colleagues, with the possible exception of the Secretary of Labor, Miss Perkins.

As early as 1939, he had fought with Secretary of State Cordell Hull and the Under-Secretary, Sumner Welles, over the policy to be pursued against Japan. With the beginning of the year 1941, he led the attack of the New Dealers against the business men. When a House investigating committee rebuked him for withholding power from the Aluminum Company with which to produce additional aluminum, it did not outwardly feaze him in the slightest. Instead, he had been harassing the President so much to let him get into the defense picture that he was finally appointed fuel administrator. He promptly turned it into a vehicle to make an apathetic populace war- and Ickes-conscious. Notwithstanding that for several years southwestern oil producers had been required by law to hold down on production to prevent flooding of the market, Ickes immediately discovered an oil shortage. It is not known what was the effect of his subsequent agitation out in the country, but in Washington it was intense.

Virtually all major industries have representatives or "institutes" in Washington. In the ensuing propaganda melee the coal and gas representatives got the jump on the oil men and for several days flooded the newspapers with suggestions that "because of the oil shortage" all smart home owners would use the summer months to replace their oil burners with other fuel systems.

When the oil people finally got their voice through the propaganda din to protest that there was plenty of oil, Ickes covered them with statements that there was enough oil but there was a shortage of transportation, because tankers had been turned over to Britain and the oil couldn't be gotten to the East. The scarcely audible statements of the railroads' representatives that they had 22,000 idle tank cars they would like to make use of made not the slightest dent in the noise.

This went on for several weeks in June and July. The daily flow of statements was likened to the snow scene in the old melodrama, *East Lynne*. Ickes began to shout ominously of gasless Sundays. Motorists becoming fearful of going on their vacations made anxious inquiries of filling-station attendants, as did newspapermen, and came to be given what seemed a uniform, well-rehearsed answer. It was:

"It isn't gasless Sundays we need, but a gasless Secretary of the Interior."

Ickes was in such high glee over his new appointment that he demanded that police patrolling Washington parks should arrest people who drove smoking cars and those who made jackrabbit starts, on the ground that they wasted fuel. He put pressure on the District of Columbia police to do the same thing. And then he sought to spread his campaign over all the cities of the East. If Mr. Roosevelt couldn't make the country war-conscious he would show him how to do it.

As the campaign of the coal and gas people to have the customers switch to their type of fuel proceeded apace, the oil distributors realized they were taking a licking. They launched a campaign urging consumers to devote the summer to improving their equipment so they would need less fuel, and the sponsors of the campaign were prepared to make these improvements at reasonable prices!

Newspapers badgered Ickes—which they liked to do —with questions of whether the orders to the automobile industry to cut down sharply on the production of the new models didn't operate against his fuel conservation crusade, in that people using their old cars would consume more gas.

All this was just an example of the confusion in Washington by which some 130,000,000 people were being moved in one direction by one department head and in the opposite direction by another.

An in-and-outer in Mr. Roosevelt's favor, Ickes did not fit in the defense plans around the turn of the year at all. Although he was the whipping boy of the presidential campaign and, in fact, had been one of the first New Dealers to launch the third-term campaign as far back as 1939, Mr. Roosevelt was not inclined to entrust any defense responsibility to him. The President was once represented by one of his friends as making it a point to listen to Ickes' every radio speech with a "mixture of amusement, approval and anxiety." For example, although the President appreciated Ickes' whooping up his indispensability, when it came to arranging for the nomination he sent Hopkins out to the Chicago convention to represent him. Ickes was in Chicago, but he was never let in on any of the plans. He and Hopkins were long-time enemies, too.

One accomplishment of the aluminum collection from the housewives was to further excite Ickes. It must be understood that each additional agency in Washington means additional publicity men. In the case of prima donnas like Ickes and La Guardia they have personal publicity staffs whose business it is to keep their boss's name in the headlines. Much of the confusion in Washington could be attributed to this battle for the headlines.

Ickes and his publicity staff chafed over the La Guardia publicity. The result was that they heightened their gasoline shortage bugaboo.

Ickes decreed overnight gasoline blackouts; subsequently, in the agitation, some filling stations were closing down for two- and three-day periods; others held customers to five gallons of gas at a time. Washington newspapers gibed Ickes; they expressed frequent doubts that he was telling the truth about a gasoline shortage. That there should be this attitude toward a cabinet official, one charged with fuel administration in times of national emergency, reflected the distrust that pervaded Washington. Naturally there was confusion. Ickes had absolutely no authority behind his gas crusade, but the big oil companies, convinced that he was moving toward rigid governmental control and eventually government ownership, were afraid of him. They sought to placate him by agreeing not to supply gas to any station that would not co-operate with him, and then they plastered the newspapers with ads, carrying Ickes' picture, in an effort to appease his vanity, and beseeching co-operation on the part of everybody. Reading between the lines of these ads, the oil operators were saying, in effect: "For heaven's sake, let's try to get along with this man!"

The Texas Company appeared in the outstanding nationally circulated magazines in August with elaborate and expensive full-page advertisements describing how many a time the motorist had found himself on a lonely road out of gas and no gas station open. This was to be no more. Always the Texaco stations would be open in rain or sunshine, darkness or light, and there was a picture of the smiling attendant in a Scott's Emulsion raincoat and hat. The advertising had been prepared several weeks before.

After Ickes went into action, Texaco carried full-page ads in the newspapers with a "correction" saying they were co-operating with the fuel administrator. It was estimated that the original and subsequent advertising cost $100,000.

One of Ickes' first orders was that the oil companies submit periodical reports of how much they spent for advertising. They shouldn't advertise when there was a "shortage" of oil, he held. But newspaper publishers remembered his frequently expressed hostility to the way newspapers were conducted.

Ickes lived on a pretentious estate about twenty

miles out of Washington in Maryland. His young wife went in for raising chickens. It had been her custom to bring the chickens into the Washington market. Ickes, by way of practicing what he preached, ruled that she must come into town at 8 o'clock in the morning and then wait until he was ready to go home at night, to save gasoline. She countered by making him bring the chickens to the market. When Ickes' picture was flashed on the screen of the Washington movie theaters in the summer, the audiences invariably laughed.

At the height of the confusion over gas, Ickes turned his crusade over to a deputy and went off on a vacation. While he was away, a Senate committee headed by Senator Frank Maloney of Connecticut concluded there was no oil shortage, and the newly created over-all agency, SPAB, denied priority on material for the construction of a pipe line from the Southwest to the East, on which Ickes and the oil operators had agreed. On his return, Ickes, considerably chastened, agreed that there was no shortage, but said there was one on the way, and he had been anticipating it. The President had left him out of the new over-all defense agency. He complained to columnist friends that nobody had been more loyal to the President or had been the "goat" for him so much. The denial of a priority for material with which to construct a pipe line was a blow to some oil companies which wanted it and had been playing ball with Ickes in his shortage agitation. Their connivance had made it impossible to get at the truth earlier.

CHAPTER XI

The Saturnalia of Billions

ONE AFTERNOON late in the summer of 1939, a group of conservative Senators—Byrd of Virginia, Taft of Ohio, Vandenberg of Michigan and Bridges of New Hampshire, as well as others—engaged in a mutual admiration session. They had just succeeded in defeating a New Deal spending bill. It was the spend-lend bill of $4,000,000,000, the defeat of which, as has been related earlier, routed the New Dealers and caused the older ones to fear that if spending were not revived in some manner the New Deal had come to the end of its rope.

Defeat of this bill was as much of a surprise to the conservatives as it was to the New Dealers. More or less perfunctorily they had launched an attack on it when it was presented in the Senate, and then, much to their amazement, they succeeded in greatly whittling it down. Then the House, which because of its organization and the fact that the members serve only two-year terms, is usually responsive to the President's wishes, particularly a strong one, did the very unexpected thing of killing the bill altogether. House members responsible for this action came over to the Senate to join with their colleagues in the impromptu celebration. It was a particular victory for Senator Byrd because for years he had been hammering away at the condition of the nation's budget.

In the midst of the celebration he warned his fellows:

"We are probably celebrating too soon. In a few weeks they will be back up here with another spending program under the guise of National Defense."

And in a few weeks, just after Hitler had gone into Poland, Mr. Roosevelt made a dramatic personal appearance before Congress. For several days the word had gone around Congress that he was going to do this, and estimates as to how much he would seek for the Army and Navy in addition to the greatly increased appropriations that had but a few months before been provided, ranged as high as $500,000,000. Mr. Roosevelt appeared, gave a graphic recital of how Hitler in a few plane jumps from Brazil to St. Louis could drop bombs on that city, and asked for one billion dollars. Senators and Congressmen chuckled at his audacity. But a few days later he asked for still another billion.

As of October 1, 1941, the amount appropriated or authorized for the defense program, including the seven-billion lend-lease bill for aid to the democracies, totaled some sixty billions, and the end was not in sight. This did not include the ordinary appropriations for running the government, totaling seven billions a year.

As of this time the strategy apparently had been

to crush Hitler with appropriations. Between July 1, 1940, and July 15, 1941, the Treasury had actually paid out under the defense program only $6,538,598,677. But the entire sum was being "obligated" as fast as the contracts could be drawn up, and by September 1, the actual spending—regular and defense—was approaching the two-billion-a-month goal of the New Dealers.

Up until September 1, the Treasury had paid out less than $400,000,000 under the $7,000,000,000 lend-lease fund, and only some $190,000,000 was for actual exports, of which $118,000,000 was for agricultural products. But several weeks before this the government propaganda mill began paving the way for another lend-lease bill of some $6,000,000,000. The advance propaganda was to the effect that British and American experts were busily engaged in working out a form of repayment on the part of the British. That repayment discussions were taking place should have afforded a pleasant surprise for the public generally. But the propaganda hastened to add that the discussions were only dealing with the broad purposes of the two governments, nothing specific, of course.

As an example of the ease with which huge appropriations were being granted, the Senate on June 27 passed the largest single money bill on record, $10,-600,000,000 for the Army, with only a score of Senators on the floor.

Thus far, however, the government officials were the greatest benefactors of the appropriations. Relatively little had been accomplished in the way of equipping an American Army or of helping Britain. When the Army chief of staff, General George C. Marshall, told Congress in July that it would demoralize the Defense Army if the guardsmen and selectees were not held in the service beyond the original one-year period, he would have been much franker had he said that because of circumstances beyond his control, they had as yet received little training under conditions of modern warfare. As Congress proceeded to debate the question in the same confusion which attended the passage of the Draft Act at the height of a political campaign, qualified commercial pilots were in some instances doing kitchen police for lack of planes, stovepipes were being used for mortars, and oak boughs mounted on forked sticks were called machine guns. Grown-up men, taken from their places of business, were running around playing hide-and-seek and saying, "Tag, you're dead, I'm a machine gun."

Congress paid little or no attention to the Army in the passage of the original draft act. Brigadier General Louis C. Hershey, who was subsequently to be placed in charge of its administration, pleaded for an age limit between eighteen and twenty-four or twenty-one and twenty-five. But there were political and other influences operating at the time over which neither Roosevelt nor Willkie had any control.

Basically, there had long been a New York group professionally and philosophically interested in permanent universal military training in this country. It was headed up by Grenville Clark, who assisted in the organization of the Plattsburg officers' training camp movement in the First World War, and who, between wars, organized an association known as the National Military Camps Association. He prepared a conscription bill and took it to Representative James W. Wadsworth of New York, who, as a Senator and chairman of the Senate Military Affairs Committee twenty years before, had sponsored universal military training. Wadsworth was a wealthy man who had given his life to politics—a gentleman farmer; his life had been pretty much on the order of the Roosevelts. Coming up through the New York Assembly, he was elected to the Senate in 1914 and re-elected in 1920. He was one of that body's ablest members. In 1926 he was defeated because he would not espouse the Dry cause. Having nothing to do, he came back to the House in 1933 and was looked upon as one of that body's ablest members, though his talents were covered under a bushel there.

An enthusiastic internationalist, although he voted against the League of Nations, he readily agreed to sponsor Clark's bill. In the Senate he persuaded Senator Burke of Nebraska, who had been defeated in the spring primaries for renomination, to co-sponsor the bill with him. Clark and Wadsworth wanted universal military training. This was a sort of hobby with them. After the fall of France in the spring of 1940, they saw their opportunity to put it across.

Then the many forces began operating. Ever since Hitler had invaded Poland, the New Dealers had made

frequent reference to the need in this country for a
"universal service" measure. In her newspaper column, Mrs. Roosevelt mentioned this need several
times. In his column in the Washington *Post,* Ernest
Lindley, New Deal journalist and White House intimate, explained that the New Dealers meant by "universal service" a system by which every man would be
required to render service and, regardless of his ability, would not receive more than the pay of an army
officer. Pending in the Senate for several years and born
of the New Deal charge that munitions makers and international bankers were responsible for wars, was a
bill by Senator Josh Lee of Oklahoma, which provided
that when men were conscripted capital should be
conscripted. He and Senator Bridges had debated the
subject on the public forum several times over a period of two years. Lee would always taunt:

"So you would conscript the men but not the dollars."

And Bridges would reply:

"You would not only conscript the men but the
property of their mothers and fathers likewise."

This, then, was the atmosphere under which the
Draft Act was considered, when admittedly there were
not the camps to house the men nor the equipment
with which to train them. Republicans, by and large,
thought it would hurt Roosevelt politically. The President remained quiet for several weeks. Then internationalist influences in New York interceded with
Willkie and persuaded him that the international sit-

uation should be taken completely out of the campaign. This was his disposition, anyway. In fact, his candidacy had originated with these same groups, which looked with holy horror upon the possibility of the Republicans nominating an isolationist and having the subsequent campaign turn upon that issue. Willkie came out for conscription in his address accepting the Republican nomination and sought to drive the Republicans in the House and Senate to support him. They wouldn't do it.

Thus, the bill as passed first by the House was strictly a political bill. The New Dealers insisted upon age limits of twenty-one to forty-five, to make it "fair" to everybody. The Army officers wrung their hands in despair, insisting they wouldn't know what to do with a man forty-five years old. Similarly, political considerations forced into the bill a one-year limitation on service and a prohibition against sending any of the men out of the Western Hemisphere. All of the debate around it, from the statements of the President down, was to the effect that it was just a precautionary measure, that under no circumstances did it contemplate any A. E. F. At the instance of Senators Lee and Bridges, the Senate reduced the age limit to thirty-one, and in conference between the two bodies the limit was made thirty-five years.

With the passage of the bill, the world was to witness, a few weeks later, on October 16, the spectacle of an estimated 16,500,000 men registering in communities all over the country, and on August 1, nine and one-half months later, only approximately 650,000 had been called for military service. They were not to be trained for war, or so they were officially told, unless Hitler came over here; they were just being sent off, apparently for the fun of it.

Only a ridiculously low percentage of them were to be called in more than nine months, yet every single one of the 16,500,000 became affected on registration day. Their employment prospects were reduced, their credit was affected; they themselves knew not how to plan for the future. For a period of several months they were held in a state of suspended animation. An employer was not likely to give a man a raise when he was facing the draft; he was not likely to employ a man facing the draft. Men whose businesses depended upon their presence naturally had difficulty getting operating credit from the banks; a real-estate operator was loath to sell a home to a man facing the draft; indeed, everybody was reluctant to extend him credit of any kind because the draft act gave the draftee considerable protection in the collection of debts.

Then some draft boards adopted the policy of not taking married men; others took them; some boards showed leniency with men over twenty-five; others inducted men of thirty-five years. Baseball players, as but an example, were inducted at the only time in their career when they had the opportunity to accumulate a competence. If one sought exemption, he risked his popularity and earning power.

In the more lenient policy of some draft boards,

large numbers of men were "rejected" because of physical defects. In her column in August, Mrs. Roosevelt had a solution for the high percentage of men rejected either by the local boards or by the Army boards. It was that they be conditioned and then enter the CCC camps. Paul McNutt, the Federal Security Administrator, had still another solution. He appointed a commission to study the percentage of those rejected, and out of this came a recommendation that the government set up a rehabilitation project. The dubious assumption was that men were hankering to get into the service.

Naturally there was confusion when Mr. Roosevelt and the Army chief of staff, General Marshall, asked Congress in July that the one-year service of the draftees be extended, and that the limitation against their being sent out of the Western Hemisphere be eliminated.

General Marshall told Congress that not to extend the period of service would disrupt his Army, because selectees would have to be brought home from as far away as Alaska and Hawaii. The fact is that only 13,806 selectees, everywhere, would have had to be discharged in November; 5,521 in December; 73,633 in January 1941; 90,238 in February; 153,159 in March; 123,207 in April; 56,896 in May, and 58,050 in June. Not more than 2,880 National Guardsmen and 2,000 selectees were in Hawaii and Alaska. And new men were being inducted all the time.

The general was named chief of staff by Mr. Roosevelt, as is usually the case, not because of his outstanding field generalship ability, but because of his political ability, the ability to get along with Congress. This is the main requisite for one in his position. But he did not help himself any in the handling of this matter. He had scarcely made his request on the grounds of a grave situation when Senator Vandenberg came into possession of a War Department order to discourage the re-enlistment of Regular Army men who had served three years. The order, signed by Major General E. S. Adams, adjutant general, at the direction of Secretary of War Stimson, said that the objection to the re-enlistment of regulars was to give untrained men an opportunity for training. Re-enlistment of regulars, the order read, was "of little benefit to the Army."

General Marshall unconvincingly explained to the Senate Military Affairs Committee that the Army wanted to be "more selective." Yet he asked for, and got, the repeal of a provision in the original draft act limiting the size of the Army.

The House, on August 12, passed the extension-of-service bill by a margin of only one vote, 203 to 202, with fourteen members deliberately not voting and with the administration mustering every ounce of strength it could command. A few days later, General Marshall announced that 200,000 men were to be released by Christmas; this, after insisting that if the service period were not extended his Army would be demoralized.

The Congressional leaders literally threw up their

hands, and in the cloakrooms uttered imprecations against the confusion "up-town." They ran their hands through their hair and wondered what their problem would be whenever another major request for legislation came from the administration. The members of the House and Senators who had voted to extend the service period felt they had been put in a false light before their constituencies, and they blamed it on lack of administrative capacity. The whole episode did not make for team work between the legislative and executive branches of government. It made for confusion.

The citizen out in the country having an opportunity to listen in on the discussions in the congressional cloakrooms would probably have been shocked at the comment called forth by the picture of Elliott and Franklin Roosevelt, Jr., in uniform with their father in his meeting with Winston Churchill. Things like this appeal to the prejudices of people, and Congressmen are close to these prejudices. Their political lives turn on them.

But after all this confusion, during which editors throughout the country took their typewriters in hand and denounced men who would not vote for the extension of service, there developed within New Deal circles in Washington a move to "demobilize" the Army with a view to concentrating on the Navy and lend-lease as this country's participation in the Second World War. The situation had changed vastly since the summer of 1940, when the need for a large Army was apparent, these influences contended. At that time, they argued, it looked as though Hitler would go through Britain and come right on over here. But now the Army was getting in the way of effective aid to the "democracies" because of the equipment it required.

The argument was first advanced, in mid-September, by the pundit, Walter Lippmann, upon whom many Senators, Congressmen and government officials depended for their thinking. But that it sprang from an influential section of the New Deal was evidenced when the semi-official columnist, Ernest Lindley, took it up. One quick accomplishment through returning the selectees and guardsmen to their homes, it was argued, was that the suspicion would be removed that Mr. Roosevelt was planning another A.E.F. It may be that this agitation was started with a view to getting the Neutrality Act repealed by Congress. This was being attempted at the time.

But it affords an amazing commentary on the way official Washington was operating. Maybe a mistake had been made, after all, in passing the conscription bill. Of what importance is a little matter like that? In Washington men have one idea affecting the lives of millions one day; the next day they have another one. People are conceived to be but pawns on a chessboard, to be moved about at will.

But these officials themselves, and their subordinates, were having the time of their lives. A weekly transatlantic ferry service was established in July to accommodate those who found it necessary to go over to London to "study the situation." Officials of the Department of Agriculture had to go over to see how the British were faring in food; those of the OPM to see how they were getting along in steel, in aluminum, in copper, in brass, in the thousand and one things with which the OPM dealt. Others had to go over to study the British morale. Every phase of British life, in fact, was being given a most exhaustive study. The extensive travel was by no means confined to officials seemingly having legitimate business. Nearly every subordinate wanted to make the trip; it was simply a question of who could get permission.

There had long been a conflict in the Department of Agriculture between the Secretary, Claude Wickard, and his Under-Secretary, Paul Appleby. Appleby, described in the various labels of Washington as a "left-winger," served happily under Wallace, but he and Wickard could not get along together.

In August, Appleby was trying to get transferred to the Federal Reserve Board.

About this time, the fellow agriculturists in the British government asked that the American Department of Agriculture send over a couple of experts to study British agricultural methods and perhaps tell them how to improve their production. Appleby was not an agricultural expert. He professed to know little if anything about agriculture. His job was that of an administrator of a vast bureaucracy. But in Wickard's absence from the city, he decided he wanted the trip, and took it.

Journalists and crusading clergymen afforded a problem to the State Department in arranging trips for them; some went over on the bombers, others on the Clipper ship. The clergymen had to go over to absorb the British spirit and come back and tell their congregations about it.

In hyperbole, it may well be that history will show one of the high points of the war to be Dorothy Thompson's emotional sweep through London.

And the British, in turn, poured in on Washington and joined with our government in ousting tenants from their apartments to make way for additional office space. There were 3,000 Britishers in the city, and the quip of the cocktail parties was: "There are more British in Washington than there were in 1812." It is true that some of them, in jovial mood and to taunt their American friends, were apt to observe when signing a dining and wining check:

"Charge this to lend-lease."

It was not illogical, of course, that their expenses came from the lend-lease administrative fund, and they had charge accounts at the restaurants and hostelries.

In September the number of government workers in Washington, exclusive of the armed forces, had risen to around 225,000, and some 35,000 additional were expected within the next few months.

In the blistering heat of midsummer, the whole city, figuratively, sat back and immensely enjoyed the spectacle of one lone man, a newspaperman and one-legged veteran of the First World War, defying the government in its efforts to take over his penthouse apartment. The government had had no designs on the building, an apartment hotel, but there were all sorts of men in town looking around for ways in which to make money. One was a promoter of no mean sort. Without any capital, he sized up the apartment hotel, learned that it could be bought, and then went and interested the Office Housing Agency of the government in leasing it. When the agency agreed, he went out looking for purchasers of the building. The fact that he had an agreement with the government to lease it for five years naturally enhanced its value. On this basis he persuaded Joseph E. Davies, whilom New Deal ambassador to Russia and to Belgium and then serving as an Assistant Secretary of State, to buy the building, some of the stock of which he gave to his son-in-law, R. L. Grosjean, a Belgian refugee.

The tenants of the building received two weeks' notice to move, and most of them did. One woman, the wife of a diplomat serving abroad, and her daughter, moved to another apartment hotel a few blocks away. Within a week the British had taken it over.

One newspaperman, George E. Ready, of the New York tabloid *PM,* raised such a rumpus, with the help of a few followers, that a committee of Congress investigated the transaction, revealed that the promoter had made at least $35,000 in commissions, besides being made president of the new operating firm, and directed the government to void the lease.

The highlight of the proceedings of the congressional investigation came when Congressman Newt V. Mills of Louisiana, a member of the committee, became angered and struck Ready. It developed that as the name of "Grosjean," Davies' son-in-law, kept bobbing up in Ready's testimony, Mills thought he was referring to the attractive Miss Grosean, who was Huey Long's secretary and whom Huey made Louisiana secretary of state.

CHAPTER XII

The Tragic Plight of Congress

CONGRESS in these days was in a state of bewilderment. It could not, or did not, function as a constructive force. When it acted at all, it was more likely to add to the confusion. Congress, as a whole, was kept in ignorance of what was going on, and even its leaders were given only such alarming information as was periodically necessary for the enactment of particular legislation.

Mr. Roosevelt had said the definite policy of this government was to crush Hitler regardless of the cost. But Congress, while showing every disposition to crush Hitler, had shown no willingness to go to the extent of sending an expeditionary force to Europe. Indeed, the extent to which this country was participating in the conflict in the summer of 1941 was almost wholly through subterfuge.

Every step thus far authorized by Congress had been authorized on the ground that it prevented a shooting war. The lend-lease bill was passed on that basis. It is true that after its passage Mr. Roosevelt proclaimed that we were not only to serve as an arsenal for democracy but to see that the goods actually got there. Yet he had given assurances to the congressional leaders, particularly to Senator Walter F. George, chairman of the Senate Foreign Relations Committee, that convoys would not be used. The President was not to become bolder in the use of the Navy for several months.

So, in spite of frequent declarations of undying support, there were limits, known to Hitler, beyond which Congress was not yet prepared to go. There were still on the statute books definite laws, not modified by the lend-lease act, prohibiting American merchant vessels from operating in the war zones. These were circumvented by Mr. Roosevelt in some instances by declaring a war zone not a war zone, and in others by transferring the registry of American vessels to small countries such as Panama. This subterfuge ran all the way down through the Washington government. It caused subordinates to seek to grab and actually to grab authority not delegated to them. Their conflicting grabs and their conflicting justifications made of Washington a bedlam of confusion.

Typical of the incidents making for suspicion and confusion was the occupation of Iceland.

One morning in early July, Mr. Roosevelt summoned the congressional leaders to the White House and gravely told them he had landed forces in Iceland to keep Hitler from seizing it. He had not had time to submit the matter to Congress. He had to act quickly. The leaders sighed and agreed, in effect, that if he could get by with it, it was all right with them.

Then the President dramatically announced the occupation to the country. And in the same breath of telling of the urgency of his action he said the troops were *subsequently* to replace British forces already there. Aside from the fact that Hitler was then occupied with Russia, manifestly the presence of British forces on the island relieved our occupation of any urgency. To add to the confusion, Premier Winston Churchill announced in the House of Commons a few days later that he had no intention of withdrawing the British forces.

It slowly dawned on members of Congress that the primary purpose of Mr. Roosevelt's action was to justify naval operations in Iceland waters. Certainly no legitimate complaint could subsequently be raised against our Navy protecting an island in which we had a stake, and we had "made a stake" in Iceland. It justified our Navy with its planes in patrolling waters pretty close to the British Isles.

The whole result of this lack of frankness was to add to the grumbling in Congress and the increasing hostility toward the administration, which was to manifest itself in a serious challenge to the request that the selectees' service be extended, and such an opposition to the Army's request for authority to send them out of this hemisphere that it was not pressed by the administration.

Such hostility, indeed, had accrued to Mr. Roosevelt's "war" moves in Congress by the late spring that the leaders advised him, if necessary, to take such steps within reason without putting any controversial questions before Congress. Newspapermen visiting Capitol Hill in quest of information were countered with inquiries by the Congressmen as to what was going on. The air was surcharged with distrust.

This does not apply to the isolationists who were openly opposing the President's moves. The surprising fact is that covert hostility came from veteran Southern members, men whose recorded votes were usually in support of the President.

It was not uncommon at all for newspapermen to be asked by such Democratic stalwarts as Congressmen Steagall of Alabama, and Rankin of Mississippi:

"Do you think the President is trying to lead us into war?"

Asked why, if they entertained these suspicions, they didn't do something about it, they explained frankly that it was political suicide for a Southern Congressman to oppose a Democratic President. If Willkie, a Republican nominee, had been elected, the Southerners said, they would have torn him to pieces on his every warlike move, with assertions that he was a tool of the international bankers and Wall Street. But they pointed to the fate of their colleagues of the First World War—Claude Kitchen of North Carolina, in the House, and Senators Hardwick of Georgia and Vardaman of Mississippi—who opposed Woodrow Wilson's war aims and were forced out of public life.

One day in late July, fourteen Senators rose in their seats to rebuke Secretary of War Stimson for having charged that their colleague, Senator Burton K. Wheeler, was near to being treasonable when he mailed out 1,000,000 postcards asking citizens to write the

President protesting against extension of the draft term. Not a single Senator raised his voice in behalf of Stimson or the President, who was inferentially under attack. The isolationists in the House and Senate were subjected to none of the experiences which dogged their predecessors in World War No. 1. Indeed, by and large, they stood high in their colleagues' estimation.

On the other hand, the most unpopular member of the Senate was Claude Pepper of Florida, the most vociferous of the President's war supporters. Earlier in the emergency he had been used by the White House to send up trial balloons, but he lost this dubious distinction as his unpopularity increased.

In the late spring he closed one of his harangues against the isolationists with a blistering attack on the America First Committee. Senator Bennett Clark, of Missouri, followed him into the Senate cloakroom and said:

"I'm getting fed up with your accusations that members of the America First Committee are unpatriotic. It so happens that my wife is active in that committee. If you keep it up, I am going to blow you clean out of the water."

There were still other members who wanted to blow Pepper out of the water, however, and in a few weeks Thomas L. Stokes, ace Scripps-Howard reporter, acting on a tip from one of these members, revealed that Pepper, acting for Millard Caldwell, a former member of Congress, and now member of the law firm with which Pepper had been associated, had intervened with Treasury procurement officials to hold up a contract for paving material at the Elgin Training Field in Florida and at the Pensacola municipal airport.

A Georgia firm, Allied Materials, presented a lower bid than the firm which Caldwell represented, Pan-American, and for which Pepper interceded. The contract called for 3,600,000 gallons of asphalt. Pepper persuaded the procurement officer, W. E. Harkness, to give Pan-American an additional order of 1,800,000 gallons as a solution to the squabble.

On August 14, a special subcommittee of the House Military Affairs Committee publicly rebuked Pepper. Its report said:

"It was apparent that Mr. Harkness had considerable feeling in the matter, and that he was aware of the fact that Senator Pepper, who had nominated him for a better job, was desirous of having an award made to Pan-American.

"The Special Committee most strongly deplores the fact that any member of Congress would permit, even by inference, an employee of the government to believe that his promotion to a better position was contingent upon the securing of a government contract by a particular corporation."

The better job which Harkness got was WPA director for Florida. Caldwell represented Pan-American on a contingent fee basis. As a result of the investigation by Stokes, a Pulitzer prize winner for outstanding reporting, and also through the investigations of Congressman Albert J. Engel of Michigan, Pepper's activities in connection with the selection and building of Camp Blanding, Florida, were revealed.

Army officers admitted that it had cost them $5,000,000 more for preparing the site alone than they had anticipated. The original estimate for the project was for $8,796,180 for 39,000 men. It was enlarged to provide for an additional 19,000 men, and the completed project actually cost $27,740,214. The camp was located forty-five miles southwest of Jacksonville on Kingsley Lake, an inland lake about two miles in diameter. Forty per cent of the building area was under lake level. When the Thirty-first Division arrived they found themselves in mud.

On about December 20, Major J. R. Rundell was appointed construction quartermaster, Major M. W. Cochran was appointed supervising construction quartermaster, and H. W. McKenzie was appointed construction superintendent for the contractor, Starrett Brothers and Eken, of New York. Payrolls immediately went down and progress went up. On February 25, McKenzie was fired on orders from General Somervell, assistant quartermaster general at Washington. With the job 86 per cent complete, Rundell was instructed to close out McKenzie as of March 15 and to make new estimates for the remaining 14 per cent of the job.

It was subsequently to be learned that Senator Pepper had brought pressure on the War Department against McKenzie.

In July 1940, two Orlando political friends of the

Senator had formed the partnership of McLeod and Wolfe, particularly to get the Camp Blanding contract for rock, neither man being able to finance it by himself. When Starrett Brothers and Eken, a New York firm, took over the construction job it was with the understanding that McLeod and Wolfe were to have the job of furnishing the rock. It was sold at $2.15 per ton. A total of 1,076,430 square yards of roadway and parkway was built with this rock at a cost of $1,247,-000. When McKenzie took over, he ordered that the paving be done with the "stabilization" method, using sand with oil and using clay as a binder, which was done at Fort Jackson, South Carolina, and other camps. With this process it was estimated that 1,076,430 square yards could have been built for $700,000.

McLeod and Wolfe also furnished some 50 per cent of the heavy equipment used in building Camp Blanding, and received between $400,000 and $500,000 in January and February. A few days after McKenzie was dismissed, McLeod and Wolfe were directed to deliver 60,000 tons of rock at $2.15 a ton to finish the work which McKenzie was going to complete with surplus rock.

A protégé of Jimmy Roosevelt's, Pepper was elected to the Senate in November 1936 to fill the unexpired term of the late Duncan U. Fletcher. Both Jimmy and Harry Hopkins with his WPA went to his support for re-election in 1938.

Shortly after coming to Washington, Pepper got married and then sent his young and attractive wife off to New York to a charm school. Thus equipped, the couple moved right into the younger New Deal social set, and in a few months they had been invited to the British embassy, which in peace times is looked upon among Washington socialites as the acme of success. The embassy makes its invitations hard to get, although it unbent considerably during the war. So Pepper was one of the very first of Washington officialdom to want to declare war. But he was virtually alone in the Senate.

It was an amazing fact that in 1941 Mr. Roosevelt and the executive branch of the Government were operating on a war basis, hauling citizens back and forth, and yet a declaration of war could not be gotten from Congress. Our Navy was operating in the Atlantic and on other seas, protecting American commerce and the commerce of our friends, when the Neutrality Act, the law of the land, specifically abandoned our traditional claim to freedom of the seas. This Neutrality Act, the President had not been able to get repealed. In late September he was laying the groundwork for a high-pressure effort to have it removed, but the outcome was in doubt. When the American steamer *Robin Moor* was sunk by a German raider off the African coast in June, Mr. Roosevelt asserted this government would not stand for that. Yet there was a law on the statute books saying it would.

For several weeks prior to the *Robin Moor's* sinking, Frankfurter and Knox had been using Columnist Alsop as a vehicle to represent Mr. Roosevelt as just waiting for an incident before taking more active participation in the war. Official Washington assumed that the *Robin Moor* constituted the incident and laughed about it.

Thus were cynicism, distrust and suspicion breeding the utter confusion of Washington. Scarcely any two groups were moving in the same direction, and no group exactly was sure that it knew whither the other was headed.

Just before the House members left for a month's vacation in mid-August, their Ways and Means Committee had finished its work on a new tax bill designed to raise some $3,300,000,000. The committee is composed of twenty-five of the ablest and most experienced members of the House, because its business is to prepare bills to raise the necessary revenue to run the government. Its work is so intricate that usually the bill it prepares is accepted by the House membership without much questioning, and then it goes to the Senate. The Constitution provides that all revenue legislation must originate in the House. The Representatives, having to come up for re-election every two years and representing districts instead of states, are closer to the people than the Senators.

The Committee thought it had done an excellent job after several weeks of hard work in preparing a bill, particularly as it had provided that henceforth married couples would have to make a joint income-tax return. Couples in the higher income brackets had been enjoying tax savings by making separate returns. A lot of agitation had arisen from people selfishly interested that the joint-return rule would cause men and women to live in sin. Other agitation revolved on the time-old crusade of women for "equal rights." Mrs. Roosevelt was interested in women's "rights," so she interceded with Mr. Roosevelt to the extent of getting him to write the venerable Congressman Robert L. Doughton, of North Carolina, chairman of the committee, saying he was vigorously opposed to the joint-return rule unless it made some saving provision for the "earned" income of a man and wife. Inasmuch as the committee didn't have time to take the bill back and work it over, the result of Mr. Roosevelt's last-minute intervention was that the House as a whole struck out the joint-return provision. For several days thereafter, newspapermen dropping into the offices of Congressmen who had favored the joint return, would find them angrily figuring out how much the elimination of the joint return provision saved the Roosevelts—the President, Mrs. Roosevelt, and the children. This was one of the things many Congressmen were doing before they left.

In July, Mr. Roosevelt asked for an appropriation of $25,000,000 for the construction of strategic highways at his discretion. Both the House and Senate, led by Representative Cartwright of Oklahoma, and Senators McKellar of Tennessee and Hayden of Arizona, eagerly responded by jumping the amount up to $320,-000,000 for a "pork barrel" distribution of "strategic" roads. Mr. Roosevelt vetoed the bill and the Senate promptly overrode his veto by a vote of 57 to 19. The

House again voted a majority for the measure, but was unable to muster quite the two-thirds majority to override a presidential veto.

Then Representative Cartwright and Senators Hayden and McKellar revived the bill by reducing it $100,000,000. The House passed it and it came to the Senate. There it was called up on an afternoon when a large number of Senators were at a ball game, making it difficult for the Senate to maintain a quorum. Under the circumstances Senator Vandenberg licked the bill again. Then he agreed to accept a reduction of but $50,000,000 and let the remaining $170,000,000 worth of "pork barrel" projects pass. Vandenberg was one of the most capable members of the Senate, but he had become tired and philosophical and clubable. He was widely reported to have walked into the Senate cloakroom after an impassioned speech against the lend-lease bill and to have said he could have made just as good a speech for the bill. He probably could have, so unconcerned had this able man become.

In anticipation of Leon Henderson's operations as price fixer, the Senate in August, at the behest of Senator "Cotton Ed" Smith of South Carolina, adopted an amendment to a pending bill providing that, regardless of what price-fixing legislation was subsequently passed, no price could be fixed for agricultural products below 110 per cent of "parity." Parity was an artificial figure that Congress had legislated for all of the major agricultural products. The Senate also provided in this "friendship for the farmer" episode that the government agencies holding wheat and cotton could not take advantage of the currently high prices to dispose of them. In addition to paying out billions of dollars in recent years in various benefits to farmers, the government had acquired millions of bushels of wheat, cotton, and other agricultural products by outright purchase or through loans, to hold up their price. Now, it couldn't even dispose of this cotton and wheat to Britain under the lend-lease transactions. Secretary Morgenthau described the Senate's action as criminal.

Confronted with Congress' mind on agriculture, the administration did not even seek to include labor wages in Leon Henderson's price-fixing bill, which it sought to pass. In the spring, when the strikes in the defense industries were at their height, considerable agitation developed in the House for legislation restricting labor unions in so far as they involved national defense. It increased by leaps and bounds over a period of several weeks, and newspaper observers came to the reluctant belief that legislation of some kind was going to be passed, though it was realized there was little likelihood of its passing the Senate. But when the House poised to take action—very tame action, at that —the CIO brought some 100 of its representatives to town from all over the country. They divided into squads and waited upon the Congressmen in force. The "anti" labor legislation was dropped.

Late in April, when Henry Morgenthau's experts were busily engaged in preparing the heaviest tax bill ever passed in this country, he tauntingly suggested that Congress pare non-defense appropriations a billion dollars. A few days later, on May 2, Speaker Sam

Rayburn of the House told a group of reporters that several members of his body had come to him suggesting that this be done, and that he planned to take the matter up with Mr. Roosevelt at the earliest possible moment. Nothing was to come of this, of course. It is doubtful if Rayburn ever mentioned it to the President, and if he did so it was as a good joke.

This was several weeks before the President had difficulty in making his veto of the $320,000,000 "pork-barrel" highway bill stick; it was before Congress was to pass the regular annual appropriation bills which continued to provide for such agencies as the National Youth Administration, the WPA, and the Civilian Conservation Corps, all of which had originated as relief projects. It was before Congress voted some one billion dollars for agricultural benefits.

Congressman John Taber of New York, a member of the House Appropriations Committee, submitted a list of non-defense items on July 31 totaling $2,146,-169,390 which he claimed could be eliminated. He said he was convinced a more thorough study could eliminate another $2,000,000,000.

There were many items which Congress would not eliminate, of course, because of administration pressure. On the other hand, there were other items which Mr. Roosevelt with his tremendous hold over that body could not get eliminated.

In the latter category were the NYA and the CCC. The CCC was given $247,000,000 for the fiscal year beginning July 1, a reduction of only $39,000,000 over the previous year. It was set up in the early New Deal days to get the youngsters of underprivileged families off the streets and out of crime. An applicant had to be between seventeen and twenty-three years of age and of needy parents. The pay was $30 a month, of which he had to send $25 home to his parents. But in 1937 the relief aspect was dropped, and vocational education—and work—were described as the main objectives of the organization. At the time there were being maintained three privately endowed lobbies in Washington paying college professors upwards of $10,000 and $12,-000 a year to worry about the plight of youth. Relief requirements were dropped by the CCC at this time; the enrollee had to be unemployed and "in need" of employment, and the CCC administrators insisted that as of January 1, 1941, 90 per cent of the enrollees were of parents who could not afford to give them vocational education. In December 1940, a group of social workers decided that the CCC training should include the melting-pot idea, instead of confining it to youngsters of the less fortunate social group. They interested Mrs. Roosevelt and Dorothy Thompson, whereupon it was agreed to make an experiment at a camp in Sharon, Vermont. Fifty CCC enrollees were placed with millionaires. After a few weeks of the experiment the recruits had gotten to the point of insisting that they be given notes the night before telling what time it was desired they should get up the next morning. J. J. McEntee, director of the CCC, a very able and conscientious administrator, reported that the millionaires were demoralizing his boys and took them back under his wing.

The NYA was established shortly after the CCC to assist young men and women whose parents had come upon evil days, to finish their high school or college educations. It moved quickly to branch over into the training field of the CCC and became a distinct rival of it. With the advent of the defense spending, its director, Aubrey Williams, who has the fanaticism of an illiterate preacher, linked his organization with the defense program, and made a more attractive offer to the youngsters than either the CCC or the Army. As opposed to the work camps of the CCC, he set up non-work "training" and "residential" centers whereby the student would be paid from $22 to $24 a month for studying to enter defense industries. He even asked Congress to grant exemption from military service for his charges. In contrast to his payments and those of $30 a month by the CCC, the Army was only paying its selectees $21 a month. Congressman Taber claimed that he had complaints from industrialists that Williams blackjacked them into giving jobs to his incompetent charges with the threat that they would be denied defense contracts unless they did so. Taber, in fact, said of the NYA:

"This outfit is a menace to the young men of the country. It tends to demoralize them and to reduce their ideals of service."

Taber, of course, was a Republican. But Williams was generally considered by Congress to be pretty much of a radical. His friends explained his fanaticism as due to his hard experience as a youngster, behind a

[232]

plow in Alabama. When he was Harry Hopkins' assistant in the WPA, he made such a revolutionary statement in a speech at Birmingham, Alabama, that Mrs. Roosevelt had to go to his rescue in the political hubbub it raised. In a subtle statement she said his intense earnestness often made him indiscreet.

In August 1941, McEntee realized that his CCC was lagging behind in the bureaucratic parade. He timidly took a step and waited to see how much political outcry it raised, before taking another. What he did was to order that the 200,000 CCC enrollees be given 15 minutes of military drill every day, five days a week. When unengaged Army officers, mostly reservists, were placed in charge of CCC camps shortly after their establishment, there were screams in Congress that the boys were going to be militarized.

In the general helplessness of Congress, one member, Albert J. Engel of Michigan, serving his fourth term, hit upon a unique way of serving his country. A veteran of the First World War, at the outset of 1941 he set himself up as a committee of one to investigate the building of the army camps. He would bob up at the camp at 7 o'clock in the morning and march in with the workers. Subsequently he would interrogate the contractors and the army quartermaster officials in charge and then make a minute inspection. Returning to Congress, he would submit his findings so dispassionately and objectively that his colleagues generally commended him. In this manner he reported what would ordinarily be considered scandals in the building of Camp Meade in Maryland, and Camp Blanding in Florida. His reports in both instances went unchallenged. In the case of Camp Meade, the old World War site was ignored by the Army purchasing officials over the protests of the contractors. The estimated cost of this camp was $9,053,187. It turned out to be $23,117,000. The selection of an entire new site necessitated dragging material through mud on improvised sleds drawn by tractors; it required all sorts of difficulties in the laying of sewers; in one instance a sewer had to be laid as deep as 25 feet, and a 1,200-foot tunnel had to be constructed from 35 to 40 feet underground, all of which would have been eliminated had the old site been chosen.

"On the one side," he reported, "I saw a ghost town where 43,000 World War troops had been cantoned and trained in 1917. The buildings were gone, but the site was still there. On the other side I saw the new camp being built on what was practically a complete new site. On the one side I saw miles of World War streets and roads, including some concrete roads leading through sites where World War buildings, barracks, etc., had once stood, and on the other side, I saw where new roads were being built at a cost of over $931,000. On the one side I saw miles of main and lateral sewer lines used in the World War, and on the other, they were spending over $600,000 constructing 146,000 feet of new sewer lines. On the one side I saw acres of level land where the old streets were laid out and where World War Barracks had stood, while on the other I saw them grading and clearing land for streets, roads and building sites at an estimated cost of $536,000."

He reported that the cost of building Fort Devens, Massachusetts, estimated at $12,474,061, turned out to be $25,188,943; that Camp Blanding, Florida, originally estimated to cost $8,796,180, was actually to cost $27,740,214; that Camp Edwards, Massachusetts, originally estimated to cost $7,240,462, actually cost more than $29,000,000. He reported that the cantonment at Indian Gap, Pennsylvania, approximately ten miles from Harrisburg, was built on seven hills, that the estimated cost was $7,665,600, while the actual cost turned out to be $17,956,027. In fact, he pointed out that the First World War cantonments for an army of 4,000,000 cost $216,000,000, of which a congressional committee after the war said $76,000,000 was wasted, while for the new army of 1,500,000 men, including the regulars in their barracks, more than $800,000,000 had already been spent up to June, 1941.

The House listened attentively to each of the Congressman's recitals, and they were duly incorporated in the *Congressional Record*, but nothing was done. Indeed, he received little or no publicity in the press.

In July, a witness before the Truman committee testified that his engineering firm, Sanderson and Porter of New York, received $1,239,000 for supervising the design, construction and first year's operation of the Army's Elwood Ordnance plant at Joliet, Illinois. The witness, Harrison Smith, a partner in the firm, was the only full-time man furnished in consideration of the fee. He said his firm had averaged

$250,000 a year for the five years preceding the defense spending. This same committee developed that the Army paid $150 a month rental for a 1917 model truck at Fort Bliss, Texas. But little press coverage, for some reason or another, was given to the hearings of the Truman committee. In late September the House Naval Affairs Committee wanted to investigate alleged exorbitant profits in naval shipbuilding, but the Navy Department was bringing pressure to prevent it from doing so.

There was little that Congress, composed of its many diverse interests and having become overwhelmed, bewildered and relatively powerless by the billions of dollars it had turned over to the executive branch in recent years, could do toward clarifying the situation in Washington. It but added to the confusion.

In the late afternoon of July 7, the House, with but a few members present, calmly passed a bill to give veterans of the First World War a monthly pension upon their reaching sixty-five, of $40 a month. The cost was estimated at $5,000,000,000. A few days later, several members, including the very able Congressman Everett M. Dirksen of Illinois, as if tired of being ignored and like spoiled boys seeking to attract attention before "company," spent several hours denouncing Lieutenant General Ben Lear, who had disciplined troops under his command for what he considered to be unruly conduct while passing a golf course. It was known as the "yoo-hoo" incident and threatened for a time to be a major issue in a Congress which collectively and individually had little comprehension of what was going on in the world or in Washington. The members were recklessly denouncing a general, too, at a time when disquieting reports were reaching Washington on the state of the morale of the selectees and National Guardsmen.

Seasoned politicians have few illusions about the durability of this country's democracy. They have seen too many corrupt city machines flourish to lay any great store by the righteousness of the citizens. Notwithstanding the scandals of the Harding administration, no national leader of the Democratic party more than momentarily entertained the thought that an outraged people would kick the Republicans out. Times were good, people were making money. And the veteran political writers of Washington had little doubt that if Coolidge had been renominated for a third term in 1928 he would have been re-elected, just as they were convinced that even had there been no collateral issues against Al Smith he could not have beaten Herbert Hoover, with "Republican prosperity" sweeping the country.

The force that prevented the third-term nomination of Coolidge, which many Washington observers thought he would like; the force that had prevented third terms in the past, was not any moral indignation of the people but the mechanics of politics, the rival ambitions, the balancing power of the politicians in Congress against the politician in the White House and his clique.

When, under the stress of the times, Congress voted Mr. Roosevelt as much money between 1933 and 1940 as had been appropriated from George Washington on down, eliminating the First World War years, it destroyed this balance. There were able and conscientious men in Congress in 1941, but as against Mr. Roosevelt they could not prevail as individuals, and Congress as a whole had come to be scarcely more than an agency of the vast bureaucracy. Collectively, it had the power to do almost anything it desired, but as long as Mr. Roosevelt had the billions to spend, and Congressmen being what they were, there was no chance of their acting collectively to recover their importance. With forces operating beyond their control, members of Congress generally were inclined to do anything to get some of the spending in their district, to get their share of the tremendous patronage which was being built up, to get the weight of the gigantic presidential power behind their re-election. It was not a case of being conscientiously for the President's foreign policy and supporting it. They bent over backwards in order not even to incur his enmity on administrative appointments against which their judgment dictated; neither did they try to help straighten out the tangled bureaucracy, or otherwise function to make the foreign policy effective.

This submissiveness was not by way of maintaining unity. It was not unity when Congress thought the nation's safety enough jeopardized to appropriate $7,000,000,000 for aid to Britain and to appropriate many other other billions to build up this nation's defense; to permit the spending of millions for Latin American good-will, to keep China fighting Japan— and then pass a bill extending the training period of selectees and national guardsmen by a margin of only one vote.

Congress by its actions and lack of action must have thought the nation's safety was enough jeopardized to permit Marriner Eccles or Leon Henderson or the OPM, or Harold Ickes to reorder and dislocate the lives of 130,000,000 American citizens, but it was seriously doubtful about the necessity of keeping 650,000 selectees and the 300,000 or so guardsmen in their camps.

Neither did Congress up to this time think the nation's safety enough jeopardized, apparently, although abundantly jeopardized, to repeal the Neutrality Act prohibiting American merchant vessels from entering the war zones, thus forcing Mr. Roosevelt to arrange for the ships to fly the flags of other and small nations such as Panama, or to declare manifest war zones, non-war zones. Neither did it think the nation's safety enough jeopardized, apparently, not to be prepared to set up an awful agitation if Mr. Roosevelt used the word "convoy" in getting the material to Britain, for which the Congress had appropriated. Congress' only willingness, apparently, was to appropriate, and the more it appropriated the more impotent it became. When Mr. Roosevelt ordered the Navy in September to shoot enemy craft on sight, helpless Congressmen giggled: "We'll send our Navy but not our boys."

This was not unity. It was a jumble of confused intellects. The tragedy of it was that the more confused they became, the less Mr. Roosevelt, being human and having his job to do as he saw it, thought of Congress. Congress was far less in Mr. Roosevelt's mind in 1941 than an administrative difficulty in one of his countless bureaus. Senator Burton K. Wheeler of Montana burned him up, but this was because he just naturally had it in for Wheeler because Wheeler had opposed him before and he credited Wheeler with keeping isolation sentiment alive. But Wheeler's influence was out in the country. He could not prevail against Roosevelt in the Senate. The President didn't have the same bitter feeling against other isolationist Senators. The Wheeler family disliked the Roosevelts and the Roosevelts disliked the Wheelers.

Also, it annoyed Mr. Roosevelt to have Senator Walter F. George as chairman of the Senate Foreign Relations Committee until he shifted to the chairmanship of the Finance Committee. Because, although George, notwithstanding he was one of the Senate's most influential and respected members, could not defeat the President on a showdown in that body, the latter had to observe certain amenities with the Senator, such as trying to explain why he, the President, felt it necessary to send marines to Iceland. It was a terrible bother for a busy man such as the President was. He didn't have to do this with the chairman of the House Foreign Affairs Committe, Sol Bloom of New

York, who liked to tell how he embarked upon his career by operating a hoochy-koochy show at the first Chicago World's Fair and now had risen to be accepted, because of his position, at the foreign embassies. Neither did the President have to give any such time and bother to Speaker Sam Rayburn of the House, or the majority leader of the Senate, Alben W. Barkley of Kentucky.

Barkley's conception of the importance of a Senator or of the "high principles" which motivate people when they vote, was given to the Senate in 1938 when he vigorously opposed a provision of the Hatch Act prohibiting the political solicitation of WPA workers. Unashamedly, he told his fellow Senators that if the WPA workers could not constitute a machine behind him he might be defeated that year because his opponent, then Governor "Happy" Chandler, since a Senator, had his machine of state employees behind him.

The smoldering indignation in Congress began to come to the surface in the first two weeks of August. The Senate Appropriations Committee, by a unanimous vote, denied a War Department request for $1,347,000,000 with which to buy special ordnance items. It was to be for a reserve pool of supplies beyond the equipment which the Army was already buying for a force of 3,000,000 men. Senator Alva Adams of Colorado, one of the Senate's economy group, led the fight for refusal of the item, but the committee as a whole felt the Army was running a good thing in the ground. It had asked for and been given $35,000,000 with which to erect a new War Department building. Then on the floor of the Senate all but $700,000,000 of the rejected item was restored.

In passing a bill authorizing the President to seize any private property needed in defense, the House insisted upon inserting a provision against the seizure of firearms from citizens, their hunting rifles, pistols and the like. Also it prohibited the seizure of any machine tools or items of manufacturing equipment which were being used in defense production. The War Department protested against both provisions on the ground that its freedom of action was limited.

The House Banking and Currency Committee, which was considering a price-fixing bill for Leon Henderson, decided in the face of the administration's clamor that no immediate action was necessary to prevent inflation, that it could wait a month, and the committee members joined with the rest of the House in taking a vacation.

Were these actions logical? Why deny the Army $700,000,000 for ordnance equipment and give it funds for a new building to house permanently 40,000 persons? Why make a stand on such a relatively unimportant matter as protecting the hunting rifles of citizens after having already given the executive branch of the government such tremendous power that no one could question its limit?

The Banking and Currency Committee's action in postponing consideration of Henderson's bill reflected a growing uneasiness in Congress over granting the power embraced in such a bill. But the committee's action was purely negative. It left Henderson to attempt to exercise the power anyway.

Congress' plight was pathetic. It was not that it supported the President in the war on Hitler, or that it would not support him. Congress' stand on this, as reflected in its actions thus far, was that it would give away the nation's substance if necessary, but "not one drop of blood" was to be shed on foreign soil. This is what the Congressmen, generally, had said in their impassioned campaign speeches. The shedding of "one drop of blood" was where Congress apparently drew the line.

The tragic thing about Congress was that in its collective bewilderment it had ceased to figure importantly in the President's or the Government's calculations. It had become so impotent that bureaucrats treated it with contempt. Seemingly it was facing the time when it would not have enough influence with the bureaucrats to get patronage or spending for its home communities.

The general public would have been surprised to know the receptivity Congressmen gave to an editorial in the New York *Daily News,* in August, suggesting the possibility that the 1942 congressional elections might be called off.

The eyes of many of them brightened at the prospect.

CHAPTER XIII

I Believe in America

DONALD NELSON, a member of the over-all defense production agency, SPAB, and later appointed as the priorities director of the OPM, a man who gave promise of being the one to bring order into the defense production set-up—in fact, one of the most orderly minds in the confusion of Washington—was once talking with a group of friends about a speech he had in mind.

How would it sound, he asked, if he said this:

"You've got to do one of two things, gentlemen: either defeat Hitler or impeach Roosevelt! You admit that the latter is impossible. Then the only thing to do is to defeat Hitler."

His auditors turned this over in their minds for a moment, and one by one, agreed:

"Donald, that is a knockout. I've never heard it better or more succinctly put."

But Nelson refrained, at least for awhile, from making that speech. Undoubtedly, he got around to giving it further analysis. The phrase did not accurately reflect his mind. He had a great personal admiration for the President, and he certainly did not think, as the phrase implied, that an American defeat of Hitler was necessary because it was a Roosevelt project and he had to be satisfied.

Nelson had to make a lot of speeches to business groups and, as he saw it, work up their enthusiasm for the defense effort, regardless of what they thought of the President. He was looking for a convincing phrase.

The significant thing is that a man in Nelson's place shared the belief of the New Dealers that American industry was not doing all it could, and that it was withholding its best endeavor from the business of defeating Hitler. Mr. Nelson is a business man and a capable one. But it is difficult to live in Washington and not look upon business as something apart from the rest of the country, as somehow constituting one entity opposed to the "people" whom the bureaucrats feel compelled to defend. The shortcomings of one Dollar-a-Year man out of the millions of people in this country engaged in one form of business or another are magnified into a collapse of business ability and honesty. There was no doubt that one could find the Dollar-a-Year ranks of the OPM honeycombed with inefficiency. There was not much inducement, the atmosphere being what it was, for the abler men to offer their services. There were similar cases of inefficiency among the men called to Washington in the First World War but they were not used as an attack on the whole capitalistic enterprise of business.

The anti-business virus, coursing through America's bloodstream ever since it took a wild stock market ride and got a hard fall, was the country's worst enemy in 1941. It was Hitler's greatest asset, as far as this country was concerned. It gave him a landing force without his having to send a single bomber or parachute troop.

Yet, the amazing fact was that business—industry—had literally wrought miracles in the year in which the defense program was seriously under way. That it had done this, in spite of steady propaganda against it, attested its sturdiness. In this period of "tooling up" tremendous readjustments had been made in the nation's industrial plants. A total of 3,429 added plants costing $4,000,000,000 had been built. Of these, 429 costing $829,000,000 had been erected with or without government assistance; 50 costing $148,000,000 had been financed by the British. The tanks, the planes, the guns were beginning to roll. Mr. Roosevelt repeatedly expressed himself as satisfied with the accomplishment, but usually added the qualification that, of course, too much could not be accomplished. The agitation came from his subordinates, the great majority of them just as sincere as any other American, but given to spouting off at the mouth about matters which they did not understand. They were largely the younger and inexperienced men. For example, Stacy May, OPM economist, spoke glibly of the necessity of getting our defense expenditures up to $3,000,000,000 a month, as if spending this much money was in itself something to be attained.

The evidence was overwhelming that the great majority of people in this country approved Mr. Roosevelt's conduct of foreign affairs. It was a conduct that so far had kept the country out of war. And in spite of the contention of the isolationists I do not believe that he has the remotest plan of sending another A. E. F. Certainly, no step in that direction has yet been taken.

There were few observers in Washington who believed, either, that Britain planned any invasion of the continent without an accompanying A. E. F. The question arose then as to what was meant by the phrase "all-out" aid, which was being so irresponsibly used. It seemed altogether logical for this country to step up its armament production, to lay down a program involving tremendous expenditures over a given time, and to put itself in a position to carry out that program. A relatively small portion of this armament was likely ever to be needed in Britain. Indeed, without an invasion of the continent, which was certainly not yet in the cards, all of this equipment stacked up over there would leave scarcely any room for the citizens.

Yet it was from this ill-defined phrase, "all-out," that much of the confusion grew. Editors and other spokesmen became impatient when oodles of armaments didn't appear immediately after an appropriation. What was perhaps more important was that it agitated the bureaucrats and moved them to over-zealousness. Many persons subscribing to the pessimism, the agitation, the statement that "industry is falling down" were, of course, malicious; others were unwitting aids of Hitler, except that undoubtedly he could see behind the hullabaloo and knew the facts.

A more ignorant statement could not be made than that which frequently was made, that this country "was woefully unprepared." It was not prepared and had not moved to prepare to invade the European continent. It was prepared to defend the Western hemisphere. Its navy was the best in the world.

The question arises, naturally, as to why one should write a book such as this at this particular time. Isn't it a throwing of a monkey wrench into the defense effort? I don't think so. Why not let's take one good searching look at official Washington? Maybe such a look will have a calming effect on the actors themselves. It is more than likely that they don't realize how they have been cutting up. They are fellow citizens, having the same ambitions, weaknesses, abilities, hopes, disappointments, joys, as the rest of us. Maybe a look at themselves in the mirror will be helpful.

And if I have sounded any despairing note in this book, it was unintentional. What I have said, and the steam, perhaps, with which I have said it, is due solely to my desire to be a reporter. The wildest and most fanatic and convincing orator could never convince me that this country will go down under the heels of an invader.

The strength of a nation is the strength of its people, not its government. Some insidious attacks have been made upon the strength of our people, and undoubtedly, we felt mentally ill after the stock market collapse. But we have indulged in the luxury of civil war, of crack-pot movements, of every conceivable political sin under the sun, without serious damage to our democratic institutions. What America needs is to keep its wits alert. The way to accomplish that is for the nation to remain calm and not permit our leaders to excite us. The hopeful fact is that we have so much national wealth that it is almost impossible for us to destroy ourselves. And no one else can do it.